Dirt Bikes 101

An introductory guide to off-road riding

Chris Carragher

©2014 Second edition

ISBN 978-0-9826335-4-0

© 2011 First edition

Chris Carragher

Printed in the United States of America. Font publisher Lantinotype (Sanchez)

Riding dirt bikes is inherently dangerous and this publication is not meant as an authoritative, in-depth guide to riding or buying a dirt bike. Each individual must do his or her own due diligence and decide if they are capable of riding a dirt bike. This book is sold with the understanding that the author, publisher, and all connected parties assume no responsibility for your safety

This book is dedicated to adventurers everywhere

Table of Contents

Preface

Preface

Thank you. By choosing this book, you've offered an opportunity to welcome you to my world. My world is one of knobby tires, pre-mix fuel, gears, sprockets and wide open spaces. You won't find any princes or princesses here—riding a dirt bike is the realm of the adventurer. Dirt bikes are a versatile breed that can purr or snarl, hurtle through the woods like a radar-blip banshee, or ramble peacefully like a lazy river. It's a great world to be part of, and I look forward to sharing it with you.

I had ridden dirt bikes on and off as a kid, but gave up riding when I "grew up". I started kicking around the idea of getting back into the sport about twelve years ago. When I decided to pick up where I left off, almost twenty years had passed since I sat on a bike and the old behemoth two stroke bikes of yesteryear had been replaced with lighter, sleeker four stroke bikes. I was totally confused when I went to buy my first adult bike, and my difficulty finding objective information, coupled with buying the wrong bike on more than one occasion was the main catalyst behind this book.

Another reason for writing this book was my concern for the way the dirt bike world had changed, sometimes for the better (the bikes) and sometimes for the worse (fewer places to ride). I began to realize the world I grew up in, the world of open spaces that offered a wealth of riding opportunities, no longer existed. Someone had unleashed the Development Monster and his voracious appetite had devoured huge expanses of land. The dirt bike community in my area had no place left to ride but a few motocross tracks. Spending a day enjoying the trails on a dirt bike was a thing of the past.

Some open land still remained, but what was once tolerated with a "no complaint, no problem" attitude was now being monitored, and trespassers prosecuted. It was a rude awakening to discover that much of the dirt bike populace had gone underground, relegated to whispers in bars, passing comments in locker rooms, private messages on discussion forums, and looking over their shoulder while riding. We need to work towards changing that scenario.

As with any journey, having a guide can make the journey easier and less costly. My goal is to point out some of the pitfalls I fell into, so you can avoid making the same mistakes. The book's aim is to help new riders decide if riding a dirt bike is something they'd like to try, and to encourage returning rides to pick up where they left off. There are many small, but important details that need to be considered before buying or riding a dirt bike.

My hope is that by reading this book you will join (or re-join) the dirt bike world as a responsible rider and help elevate our community on par with other recreational users. To accomplish that, you'll need to make informed decisions about safety, noise, legal riding areas, and proper bike choice. Dirt bikes aren't for everyone, but for those willing to give it a try, you'll find a long, winding adventure-filled road waiting. Thank you for allowing me to be your guide.

> Riding as a kid was fun, but riding as an adult is an absolute blast because I can appreciate it more!

Chapter One:
Introduction

"The tragedy of life is not that it ends so soon, but that we wait so long to begin it." W.M. Lewis

Humans love flirting with danger. We start at an early age and never seem to lose our love/fear relationship with the angst-monster within. We swing on swings, climb in trees, ride insanely fast roller coasters, and jump off nose-bleed high bridges with nothing but a rubber band saving us from death. We crave action and adventure—damn the torpedoes and full speed ahead! Riding a dirt bike fulfills this craving for an adrenaline rush, but we can control (to a certain extent) whether we ride at panic-attack speed or just spend time outdoors enjoying a trail ride.

Chapter One

If you've never ridden a dirt bike before, it might be difficult to understand the enchantment. The sense of freedom, power, and uninhibited joy are only part of the equation. The physical and mental challenge, the sense of accomplishment, and the thrill of flirting with a measure of danger all add to the allure. It combines the "group hug" family fun with the "smack-the-hornet's-nest-and-run-like-Hell" kind of fun. From a practical standpoint, riding a dirt bike keeps you in great physical shape, teaches (or reinforces) motor skills (think Alzheimer's), and finally, it's a great way to meet new people and spend a day outdoors with family and friends,

Dirt Bikes 101 was written for new adult riders, as well as those who may have ridden as a kid but haven't been on a dirt bike for decades. The goal is not to re-capture your youth; you're an adult with adult responsibilities. The goal is to help lay out a plan that will keep you happy and safe. Sometimes adult worries insinuate their way into our lives and we end up worrying ourselves into inertia. Moderation and common sense are key components to getting yourself safely into (or back into) the saddle. Many of the dangers inherent with dirt bikes can be mitigated with proper planning, appropriate safety gear, and a well thought-out approach.

Who This Book Is For . . .

It's for adult beginners who have little or no experience with dirt bikes. We won't teach you how to ride a dirt bike, but we'll point you in the right direction to help you learn, whether you've never ridden before, or if you're out of practice. You'll gain a better understanding of the many aspects of owning a bike, which will enable you to make educated decisions should you decide to give off-road riding a try.

It's also for street bike riders who have always wanted to ride dirt bikes (c'mon, admit it). Street riders have a leg up over those who have never ridden a bike before, but there are many important differences (seat height, center of gravity, absence of road rules, etc.) between riding a street bike and riding a dirt bike that you need to be aware of in order to make a safe transition from street to dirt.

And finally, it's a book for fettered spirits looking for an oasis in a Big Box world full of project deadlines, long commutes, and office politics. It's just you, the bike, and those moments in time.

. . . And Who This Book Is Not For

It's not for parents looking to get their kids started with dirt bikes. There are too many variables with kids and ultimately it's a parental decision. A word of caution for parents though—just because you've ridden dirt bikes back in the day does not mean your child wants to ride. Take your cue from him/her and let it play out from there. If your son (or daughter) knows the stats of the top motocross racers but isn't sure which team won the Super Bowl, or if he runs around the house making "vroom" and braaaap" noises, or insists on having his toy dirt bike at the dinner table, chances are he's got the bug.

It's not for experienced riders. You won't learn the secrets to blitzing a whoops section, shaving your lap times, or popping wheelies. Mechanics won't find any tips for installing a jet kit, setting the sag, or dialing in a suspension.

Although the book is aimed at beginners, it's not an in-depth how-to-ride book. We'll touch on who to contact if you've never ridden before and offer a few book/DVD and website resources, but it's beyond the scope of this book to delve into the finer points of how to ride a dirt bike. And finally, it's not a where-to-ride book. We'll offer suggestions for finding places to ride and starting an off-road club, but we won't cover any specific trail systems.

A Toe in the Water Approach

Any new endeavor requires basic study and learning to ride a dirt bike is no exception. If you stick with anything long enough, time and experience will give you confidence to tackle more difficult tasks, meaning don't expect to be a competitive motocross racer right away if you haven't ridden for 20 years. Start in your backyard and take it from there. You wouldn't go out and build a house without first building smaller projects like decks and additions, and doctors don't start their career with open heart surgery. Start slow and work your way up.

You'll need to be in somewhat decent shape before you start riding. You don't need to be a triathlete, but if you're a total couch potato, you're going to suffer, just as you would if you took up tennis or snowboarding without exercising for a few months (at least) beforehand. A combination of moderate aerobics (running, cycling), strength exercises (weights, isometrics) along with some stretching will make a big difference.

When you were young it was all about you, and you could do as you pleased. Now that you're an adult, you no longer have that option because your family depends on you, and the bank expects their mortgage and car payment every month. Adulthood shouldn't feel like a prison sentence, but you need to balance personal enjoyment with adult responsibilities.

Adults are aware, sometimes achingly, that Time is finite, fleeting, and very, very valuable. Keep in mind that the shifting sands of time will move with or without you, and a common sense approach is all you need to yield many years of happy and safe riding. Be smart, be safe, and your only regret will be having waited so long to start riding.

Steps to a Common Sense Approach:

- research, research, and research some more
- visit local tracks and/or off-road parks
- buy the proper safety gear
- make friends with other riders, either in person or via the Internet
- if you're not physically active, begin an exercise or cardio program
- talk over your plans with your family
- prioritize your spending—dirt bikes are toys and should not break the household budget
- be sure you have an acceptable (legal and safe) place to ride your new bike

- buy the correct bike and ride within your skill level

Chapter Overview:

Preface

Chapter One: *Introduction* - Is this book for me? What can I expect? What topics will you cover?

Chapter Two: *Safety First!* - What type of gear do I need? Aren't dirt bikes dangerous? What if I've never ridden before?

Chapter Three: *Practical Aspects* - Where can I ride? How much land do I need? Does my bike need to be registered?

Chapter Four: *Noise* - What if my neighbor complains? Why are some bikes noisier than others?

Chapter Five: *Which Bike?* - What type of bike should I get? What's the difference between a two stroke and four stroke?

Chapter Six: *Narrowing Your Choices* - Yamaha, KTM, or Honda? How do I know which model is which?

Chapter Seven: *A Few Words for the Ladies* - Will I fall? Am I too short? Do they make safety gear for women?

Chapter Eight: *Clubs Are Essential* - Should I start a club? How do I get started? What are the benefits of a club?

Chapter Nine: *The Future of Off-Road Recreation* - In the Struggle for Existence, how are dirt bikes going to survive? What's our plan? Can we adapt, or will be exterminated by other recreational species?

Chapter Ten: **A Few Basic Riding Tips** - Just bought a new bike? Need a few basic riding tips to get you started?

Chapter Eleven: *Glossary* - What is a tabletop? What are whoops?

Chapter Twelve: *Resources* - What magazines can I subscribe to? What about off-road websites? Books and DVD's?

Chapter Two:
Safety First!

"The idea is to die young as late as possible."
Ashley Montagu

Riding a dirt bike definitely involves an element of danger, so we will begin with an overview of basic safety gear. For those who feel safety gear is too expensive, ask yourself what your body is worth and how much it would cost to be out of work for a few months. Only teenagers are invincible and will live forever—adults are mere mortals and will need safety gear.

Kids bounce, adults break; enough said.

Safety Gear Recommendations

Helmet: At the very least you'll need a DOT (Department of Transportation) approved off-road specific helmet that offers full face protection. Don't use an open-face street bike helmet when riding off-road. You'll need the addition full-face protection for the many times you're going to be hitting the ground. You'll also appreciate the full-face protection the first time your chin unexpectedly hits the handlebars.

A helmet with a Snell rating means it has gone through additional testing and offers more protection than one with only a DOT rating, and is worth the extra money. The back of the helmet should have a tag/sticker that says either DOT or Snell DOT. If you're buying a used helmet (really bad idea) and it doesn't have those tags, don't buy it, no matter what the seller tells you. Remember the saying—if you have a ten dollar head, buy a ten dollar helmet. A good quality helmet is a crucial piece of safety gear. Don't skimp!

Goggles: Whether you ride motocross or off-road, goggles are a smart choice. Bodily injuries are painful, but most can be repaired (broken bones, torn ACL, losing a tooth), but eye injuries aren't as easy to repair. On a motocross track, mud, dirt, and small rocks are everywhere. Off-road trails are even worse with Mother Nature doing her very best to keep us on our toes by constantly rearranging the landscape. Bugs, dust, mud and rocks can wreak havoc if they get in your eyes and might cause you to lose control of the bike.

Goggles come in many styles and sometimes your wallet is the only deciding factor. Most decent goggles offer some degree of UV protection, anti-fogging treatment, and sweat absorption foam. A few goggles even come with a tiny fan powered by a AAA battery to keep the inside of the goggles from fogging up. If you wear prescription glasses, look for OTG (Over the Glasses) goggles which are bit larger than the regular goggles. Also make sure you're buying adult-sized goggles, not youth size. If you can't afford anything else, cheap goggles are better than nothing, but the lenses scratch very easily (been there), and will eventually get bad enough to start obscuring your vision. Always keep your goggles (cheap or expensive) in a goggle pouch or at least wrap them with a soft cloth.

In an eye vs. twig fight, the twig is going to win every time, so get a decent pair of goggles. Remember: there are no eye wash stations out in the woods.

Tear-offs and roll-offs: Tear-offs and roll-offs are used to clear mud off your goggles. Tear-offs, which mount to a post on either side of the goggle frame, have been around for decades but are slowly being replaced by the roll-off system, which also mount to the goggle frame but uses a spool of film that advances via a mechanism (ratchet, string, etc.). They're not outrageously expensive and are a good idea for those riding on muddy tracks or trails.

The reason tear-offs are being replaced is partly due to environmental/manpower issues, and some tracks no longer allow their use. When you have hundreds of riders peeling off the non-biodegradable plastic lenses along the track, it makes a huge mess. Even if you're out on the trail with just a few friends, you don't want to leave any garbage behind. Some people are just looking for another reason for dirt bikes to be banned from shared-use trails. Go with roll-offs instead.

If you do decide to go with tear-offs, when purchasing your first set make sure the posts are included—replacement sets don't normally include the posts, just the lenses. When purchasing roll-offs, make sure the set you're purchasing will fit your goggles. Many of the roll-off systems are universal, but some are proprietary and will not fit another style of goggles.

Gloves: Sweaty, numb, or muddy hands don't grip controls well. Hand guards offer some protection from the mud, but gloves are a good extra layer. Sometimes a trail ride lasts longer than planned and if the balmy autumn afternoon turns into a frigid evening you'll be grateful for the extra protection.

Boots: This may seem like an expensive piece of gear for beginners, but the first time you fall (and you will fall) you'll be glad you spent the money. Those mufflers get hot and if the bike should land on your leg, it will easily singe, scald, or even burn your skin. Boots will help protect your ankle if (it's more like when) your foot catches on a berm in a turn and gets wrenched sideways. Boots also protect your shins from kick starters that spring back and bite you (sounds wimpy but it hurts).

Choosing an off-road boot is not easy. Gaerne, Alpinestars, MSR, and Fox all make excellent boots but there are many small differences in each fit and the only way to find the right boot is to try them on. MX boots don't come in as wide a range of width choices as shoes—it's a size 10 and that's it. There are small differences in the cut of each boot and since humans come in such a wide range of sizes, it's no wonder it's so hard to find the right boot.

Boots are a great investment and will last many years but be careful the first few times you wear them. They take a bit of getting used to, especially when shifting gears. It's best to try them out on a few short, quiet rides before hitting any difficult terrain.

If you decide to forego the motocross boots, at least wear over the ankle work-type boots. Wearing sneakers is always a bad idea, especially for beginners.

Jersey and pants: you can ride in jeans (no shorts!) and a tee shirt but if you have the money, invest in some off-road specific gear. It's designed for off-road riding so it doesn't restrict your movements and has extra padding in all the right places to help keep abrasions to a minimum. Pants especially are a good investment. Jeans are okay, but they seem to have seams in all the wrong places. Not only is that uncomfortable, but it can wear the seat down. MX pants are tapered on the bottom to fit inside a pair of boots so you're not crushing the folded-over jeans leg against your calf muscle. You'll also look super cool stopping in the convenience store on the way home from the trails decked out in your colorful MX gear!!

Neck brace: Leatt neck braces have been around the mainstream MX scene since about 2005 and if you look at the top pro riders today you'll notice most are wearing a neck brace. Neck injuries (like eye injuries) are not as easy to fix as broken bones, and they have the potential to do permanent and debilitating damage. Is a neck brace overkill for a beginner? They're not cheap, and there are tens of thousands of riders out there riding without one, but in the end only you can make that decision.

A **chest protector** is a good idea, particularly for those riding in rocky areas. **Knee braces** are also a smart choice, especially if you're headed to the motocross track.

It's not considered safety gear to most people, but a **hydration pack**, which allows you to sip water through a straw as you're riding, is another smart piece of equipment especially if you live in hot, arid regions. Riding a dirt bike is physically demanding and if you're not used to the exertion, you may not realize how much energy and body fluids you're expending.

And finally, for those headed out to the trails, a small backpack, fanny pack or **fender pack** is a useful piece of equipment to carry emergency supplies such as a cell phone, snack bar, bottled water, multi-tool, roll of tape, and copies of the bike's paperwork (if your trails require). If you're taking your smartphone along consider getting some added protection for it in the form of an Otter Box cover.

Visit some of the off-road stores listed in Chapter Twelve and look through the protective gear section to see all your options. Only you can decide where to draw the line as far as what gear to buy.

> Remember: the most important piece of safety gear is sitting on your shoulders - protect it at all costs!

Once you have the basic safety gear, the next step in your journey will depend upon your level of riding experience.

But I've Never Ridden Before!

Fear not! Nobody was born being able to ride; we all had to learn and you can, too. Learning to ride a dirt bike as an adult is more difficult than learning when you were a kid, but that's true of any sport.

There are several courses of action a beginner can take, but the best option by far, is a safety course. The Motorcycle Safety Foundation (MSF) offers two Basic Rider courses: the MSF Basic Rider Street Course for street bikes, and the MSF Dirt Bike School. The dirt bike school might make more sense, but the street bike course has its own set of advantages:

- the Basic Rider Street Course is offered in many more locations than the Dirt Bike School
- in most states the BRSC waiver is accepted in lieu of a road test (but be sure to check with your State's DMV to be sure)
- a street license will allow you to ride dual-sport events, (enduros) which can expand your riding opportunities
- if you don't have a place to ride dirt bikes, you can gain some experience riding on pavement instead
- riding a street bike in a controlled environment is a good way to find out if you feel comfortable piloting a motorcycle—if you feel overwhelmed on the smooth pavement, off-road riding is probably not for you

Either safety course is a great way to begin your off-road adventure. There is, of course, the age-old school of hard knocks. The fly-by-the-seat-of-your-pants school will work, but is best left for those who have their own property. Public trails are not a good venue for this type of schooling, and be absolutely certain your insurance premiums are paid up to date!

But I've Ridden Before!

If you decide to forego the safety course because you have some experience, your best bet is to start looking for off-road clubs in your area. Even if you have enough property to ride on, clubs are a great source of help and information about proper gear selection and which bike would be best for the local terrain. The club's members are dedicated to the sport, know the rules, and sometimes organize events like harescrambles and enduros. They may have a member-only riding area as well. Ask if they need volunteers for any events or work days as it's a great way for you to meet other riders. Working race events will give you a firsthand look at what racing is like, and you can decide if you'd like your riding to head in that direction.

We haven't yet discussed details of buying a bike, but if you already have a bike or someone is willing to lend you one, congratulations! Take the bike out for a few easy laps until you get a feel for the throttle, clutch and brakes. Even if you only go around your yard in small circles, at least you will become familiar with the way the bike handles.

It's true that you never forget how to ride a bicycle or a dirt bike, but riding a dirt bike is not as simple as riding a bicycle. You can get hurt much faster on a dirt bike than on a bicycle, so start slow and be cautious of other riders, especially if you'll be riding on shared trails. Public trails are just that— public; and are not the best location to re-learn old skills.

No matter how experienced you are, whenever you get on an unfamiliar bike, be sure to familiarize yourself with the controls. Most bikes are set up with the clutch lever on the left and the front brake lever on the right (as you're sitting on the bike). An easy way for new riders to remember this is that the cLutch is on the Left and the front bRake is on the Right. The rear brake is controlled by the right foot, and the shifter is controlled by the left foot, with the shift sequence being shift down for first gear, then for neutral and the higher gears, shift up.

Anyone who has ridden a bicycle knows that grabbing too much front brake will make the rear of the bicycle fly over the front end of the bicycle, and the same is true of a dirt bike. Apply both brakes evenly and you'll be fine. Your best bet is to put the bike up on a bike stand and practice with the controls to get familiar with the bike before you actually fire up the engine.

Even though most levers and shifter locations are standard, each bike has a different feel. For safety's sake, start off slow in an out of the way area until you feel comfortable. Try to find a large flat area with good loamy soil and no obstacles to run into. Practice until you feel like you're in control. Today's bikes are powerful machines and if you grab too much throttle too quickly, they will spit you off in a heartbeat. Remember—safety first!

Trail Etiquette

Keep in mind there are not always rules out on the trails, and even if rules exist, there are not always enough rangers around to enforce them. Inconsiderate riders, mud, ruts, downed trees, low branches, wildlife, hikers, cyclists, equestrians, rock slides, rain gullies, washouts and the ubiquitous ATV all present potential problems to dirt bikers. This isn't meant to scare or discourage you, just make you aware that you need to pay attention at all times. Proper trail etiquette and safety go hand in hand, so this list is being included in the chapter on safety.

Basic trail guidelines: Here are some basic rules to keep in mind on any track or trail, whether public or private:

- pay attention to, and obey all signage
- whether the trails are one-way or two-way always keep to the right, especially if you're a beginner and might be travelling slower than the average rider
- it's up to a faster rider to navigate around a slower rider, so if a faster rider comes up and wants to pass, don't panic; stay to the right and keep travelling in a straight line at a steady, comfortable speed
- when riding with friends, do not take up the entire trail; travel single file if necessary, and always travel single file on a turn
- do not stop in the middle of the trail for any reason, especially if you're on a turn
- if your bike breaks down, drag it to the side of the trail
- if someone is hurt, get another rider to slow the oncoming traffic until help arrives
- carry a fanny pack or fender pack with your emergency contact information and some emergency supplies
- leave an itinerary with family or friends, so if something does go wrong, they can tell the authorities where to find you

- stay on the trail and travel at a speed that's comfortable for you and keeps you in control of the bike
- don't carry passengers if the bike is not built for that purpose
- don't ride alone—you may get lost or stranded and cell phones don't always work out in the woods
- don't follow the rider in front of you too closely, especially at higher speeds—you might stay in control but if they don't, you risk running them over or crashing into them
- off-road trails and motocross tracks are not day care centers—you are responsible for your kids even if they ride better than you do
- some places might not allow smoking except in designated areas due to the surrounding woods and fear of forest fires
- check the weather report before you leave your house and pack extra water if it will be hot, or extra clothing if it will be cold
- get into the habit of going over the bike to make sure nothing is broken
- it should go without saying, but riding while under the influence of drugs or alcohol is not only illegal, it's idiotic—if you don't get a

rush from riding a dirt bike, get your blood pressure checked!

> You are responsible for your safety and the safety of others at all times.

Basic Pre-Ride Checklist

Even if your bike is new, performing a pre-ride check before hitting the trails is a good habit to develop. Once you've done it a few times it won't take long. Here are some of the basics:

tranny oil	....	no leaks, level correct
coolant	....	no leaks, level correct
clutch	....	functions properly
air cleaner	....	cleaned and oiled
tires	....	correct pressure
spokes	....	none loose or bent
chain	....	oiled and correct slack
throttle	....	grip returns smoothly
handlebars	....	do not bind on cables
sprocket	....	no wear or damage
forks	....	no oil leaks

The Motorcycle Safety Foundation also has a pre-ride checklist which uses the acronym T-CLOCS as a way for riders to formulate a consistent plan for checking over the bike. Your bike may not have all the components (i.e. side stand, lights and electric) shown in the list, but you can customize your own checklist to suit your particular bike. The list was created with street bikes in mind, but you get the idea—look over your bike before every ride.

T-CLOCS

T = **T**ires and wheels including spokes and tire pressure

C = **C**ontrols: levers, switches, cables, hoses, throttle

L = **L**ights and electrics

O = **O**il and other fluids (radiator, tranny, brake)

C = **C**hassis

S = **S**ide stand

In addition to mechanical maintenance, try to wash your bike after every ride (get a plug for the exhaust before you do), and buy a spare air filter so you'll always have a clean one on hand and ready to go.

Familiarize yourself with your owner's manual so you can stay on top of the routine maintenance. If you decide to buy a used bike and it doesn't come with an owner's manual, try to find one on the Internet as soon as possible to be sure your bike is safe and ready to ride.

One other safety item is for those who may decide to give motocross a try. You'll need to know what the flags mean when on the track, so they're being included in the chapter on safety. The flags are fairly consistent from track to track but sometimes have slightly different interpretations. For instance, at all tracks the yellow flag means caution, but some tracks allow you to pass while others do not. It's up to you to find what the flags mean at your track. Ignorance is no excuse!

Motocross Flags:

- *Green:* race is a go, all is good
- *Yellow:* exercise caution
- *Black:* leave the race track and find an official
- *White:* one lap left to go
- *Checkered:* you've finished the race (hopefully you've won)
- *Red:* stop all racing and stay in that spot until directed by a track official on where to go

- *Blue/orange:* move to the outside of the track
- *White/Red Cross:* ambulance and/or medical personnel on track, rider injured; slow down and maintain your position, no passing or jumping

Although buying safety gear is the most important step, there are many other considerations to take into account before actually buying a bike as we will see in the following chapter.

Chapter Three:
Practical Aspects

Buy land—they ain't making any more of the stuff."
Will Rogers

Soooooo . . . you wanna buy a dirt bike. It sounds easy enough: research different bikes, head to a dealer, hand over your credit card and *viola!* you own a dirt bike. You get the bike home, start riding around your property and the next thing you know, a police car is pulling into your driveway. Uh oh! One of your neighbors is a very unhappy camper.

Before buying a dirt bike, there are a few important details to take into consideration. You may decide it isn't worthwhile to buy a bike because there is no convenient place to ride, or if you planned on riding in your yard, you may find your neighbors won't tolerate the noise or dust in their neighborhood. Unfortunately, not everyone likes dirt bikes.

Swinging Your Arm

America is a great country founded on individual freedom. Based on that foundation, we feel entitled to enjoy what rightfully belongs to us (our property). Well ... kinda, sorta. You own your arm and are entitled to use the space around it, but the right to swing your arm ends where the other person's nose begins. It's loosely similar with your property. You've earned it, you own it, but unless you live on your own island somewhere, that property is part of a neighborhood, and a town, and a state, and a country, and a society. In other words: it's not all about you.

Everyone else is entitled to enjoy their home and property, as well. It's where friends and family reconnect, and it's our safe haven from the rapacious clutches of everyday life. The noise and dust from your bike isn't stopping at the property line. Even though it's your property, like it or not, you need to take your neighbors into consideration if you are planning to ride a dirt bike in your community. For those fortunate enough to own a large parcel of property you will encounter few, if any, neighborhood issues. But if you're like many people living on smaller acreage in modern suburbia, you'll need a little forethought up front in order to save yourself a lot of headaches and bitter feelings later.

Five acres is more than enough property for a small backyard track, but is that five acres in an area of $600,000 homes with Beemers and baby Hummers in the driveway? What's the topography and road frontage of the property? Are the houses right next to each other? Is there a wooded buffer zone between houses, and if not, can you plant one? Does your neighbor have a swimming pool or entertain outdoors frequently? The biggest question of all is: are you on friendly terms with your neighbors? If your neighbor isn't happy about the noise and the dust, you're not going to be happy either. Chapter Four goes into more detail about noise and riding in residential areas.

But Where Can I Ride?

If your property is too small for a backyard track, or if you have hostile neighbors, you'll have to look elsewhere for a place to ride. "Elsewhere" meaning a legal riding area, but no book on dirt bikes would be complete if it didn't touch on the troublesome subject of illegal riding, also known as trespassing.

(Not So) Tolerated Areas

There are still many pockets of vacant land that checkerboard across neighborhoods throughout the country. Some parcels interconnect and create a labyrinth of trails, some are empty fields, and some locales have a system of high tension power lines that are used as trails. These areas are loosely referred to as "tolerated areas", meaning the authorities will tolerate people riding in these areas taking a "no complaint, no problem" attitude.

Tolerated areas used to be, and in some cases still are, local secrets that have managed to survive in part because only the locals knew of their existence. With the advent of discussion forums and mapping sites such as Google Earth, these small pockets of real estate have become public knowledge and are quickly becoming endangered areas due to overcrowding.

Most tolerated areas are relatively small and usually only support the local population of riders. When too many dirt bikes and ATVs congregate in a small area, especially an area without a place to park the non-local vehicles, the complaints are sure to follow. If you see dirt bikes or ATVs being ridden around a particular area when you drive by but don't see any vehicles parked anywhere, it's a good bet there's a local riding spot nearby. Don't go there without one of the locals—you're just a police magnet if you park along the road. Very often, local non-riding residents are willing to tolerate local riders but won't tolerate outsiders. If having a place to ride is important enough to you, talk to a real estate agent and tell them you're interested in buying a house in that neighborhood; then you'll be a local.

When you buy a dirt bike you're only buying the bike, not deeded access to someone else's property. If you decided to take up scuba diving, would you use your neighbor's pool to practice in without permission? The same principle applies to trespassing with a dirt bike. You didn't pay for the land, it doesn't belong to you, and you don't have permission to be there. Just because no one is screaming at you when you ride by doesn't mean they aren't on the phone with the police or town supervisor. Please don't buy a dirt bike unless you have a safe, legal place to ride.

Many people have difficulty adjusting when their world changes. If you're a returning rider and had a local place to ride for years when you were a kid but now the local law enforcement says you can't ride there anymore, do as they say. We need to realize we are all ambassadors for the sport and if we continue to trespass it makes us all look bad. Be grateful for all the years you were able to ride there, and find another place to ride.

Legal Riding Areas

Fortunately, there are many legal trail systems, tracks, and off-road parks to choose from. Research the options in your state and you'll probably find a good selection of places to ride. The three main riding areas are: motocross tracks, public trail systems, and private off-road parks. Tracks, trails, and parks all offer a wide variety of challenges and fun for every rider and skill level.

Motocross tracks: If you're lucky enough to have a motocross track nearby, investigate their open practice days. Open practice days are not races; they are a time when the track is open for everyone to practice ride, and everyone enjoys the track at his or her own pace. Even if you're not interested in racing, riding at the track gives you another place to ride, introduces you to other riders, and will improve your riding abilities. Whatever you do though, don't get caught up in the skill set of the other riders. Ride within your limits! Those guys (and sometimes gals) that you see flying around the track were once a beginner and were standing where you are now. At some point in the future you'll be riding alongside them, and another newbie will take your place as the slow rider, so don't rush it.

Motocross tracks are filled with jumps, but if you feel intimidated, you don't have to jump the jumps right away. You can simply roll across them at a slow speed until you begin to feel comfortable and gain some confidence. After a few laps you may want to try a jump and the safest jump to try (if there is such a thing as a safe jump) is a tabletop. Jumping a dirt bike is always dangerous, but misjudging your speed on a tabletop is slightly less dangerous than misjudging your speed on a jump with an inclined face since you're more likely to land on flat ground, not on the incline or decline of a sloped jump. Take your time, and ride within your limits and confidence. Your family wants you back in one piece at the end of the day. Safety first!!

Each track has its own rules and regulations so be sure to find out what they are before going. They may require that you tape over the headlight and remove the kickstand (if your bike has them). Spend a day at the track as a visitor and take note of what type of equipment other riders bring.

You'll need a lawn chair, food, water, bike stand, fuel, oil, rags, raingear, etc. Find out if your local track has a website with a discussion forum. Forums are a great way to interact with other riders.

When you first join the forum, take time to introduce yourself just as you would if you met someone in real life. Tell everyone you're a beginner interested in learning more about riding at the track. Eventually ask if someone might be willing to accompany you on your first ride at the track so you can learn about the proper etiquette and safety procedures. You'll probably have several volunteers and remember: once you're an experienced rider don't forget to return the favor to the next beginner.

Public trails: If you don't own sufficient property and there are no motocross tracks nearby, look into your State's public trail system. Investigate the existence of any trail systems in your State before buying a bike, because some States have a wealth of well organized trail systems while others have nary a one. If there are trails but none are local, decide how far you are willing to travel to get to the trails. Remember—you'll need to load the bikes and gear, drive to the trails, unload, ride, reload the bikes and gear, and drive home. A two hour drive in the morning when you're fresh and excited is easy. It's the two hour drive home after a long day of riding that can be tough.

Research the particulars of each trail system, such as hours and days of operation, registration and insurance requirements, and whether it is a multi-use trail system (shared with horses, cyclists, or hikers). If it's shared with other users, be sure to yield right-of-way, especially to equestrians. The noise of the dirt bike can scare the horses and they may spook (jump sideways), causing the rider to fall. Many trail systems, particularly those in the northeast, close down for the winter since the off-road trails are often used by snowmobilers so you may not be able to ride your bike all year long.

Private tracks: Supply and demand drives our free market economy. As the popularity of off-road riding soars, the demand for off-road riding areas will continue to increase, and new privately owned parks will open across the country. "Build it and they will come" doesn't apply only to baseball stadiums. Most private parks encompass large acreage and offer some combination of track and trails. They often have on-site cabins or camping, shower facilities, a restaurant or snack bar, pro shop, bike rentals, and sometimes instruction, especially for beginners.

Private parks tend to police their trails better than public areas, making it safer for all riders, and many parks have a separate area set aside for kids and beginners. Just as with your State's trail system, the number of private parks varies by location. Investigate the parks in your area before buying a bike to be sure that you have a safe and legal place to ride.

Registration and Insurance

Registration and insurance laws for dirt bikes vary by State but the bottom line is: why wouldn't you register your bike? Dirt bikes are easy to steal and registering the bike proves ownership. Insurance for off-road bikes is usually not mandatory, but the insurance cost is much less than for an automobile. Each trail system has their own requirements so check with the governing agency before hitting the trails, but it's safe to say most agencies will require at least a registration. Some States offer reciprocity so be sure to ask. Reciprocity is when one State recognizes and honors the registration of another. You may still have to pay a daily use fee to the reciprocating State so investigate the particulars before heading out to unfamiliar trails. Most motocross tracks and private parks only require riders to sign a waiver.

Transporting the Bike

Transporting your bike is a necessity if you can't ride on your property, or if you want to ride a public trail system for a nice change of pace. The three main transportation options are pickup trucks, trailers, and hitch receiver haulers.

Pickup trucks: If you have a pickup, you'll need a ramp. The drawback to the pickup truck is the loss of storage space for gear and the steep angle of the ramp. Getting the bike up and down that ramp can be tricky, so getting two ramps, one for you and one for the bike might be a better option until you get the hang of manipulating an unwieldy and uncooperative bike up and down the ramps. Wooden ramps can be slippery, so use caution in the wet weather. Placing anti-slip strips along the length of the ramp is a good idea.

If you're still struggling with loading or unloading the bike using the single ramps, you might try one of those tri-fold ramps that are made for loading lawn tractors and ATVs. Be sure to follow the manufacturer's directions for securing the ramp to the truck. One tip to keep in mind when loading the bike regardless which ramp system you use: be committed! Don't stop half way up the ramp or you're sure to lose footing and drop the bike.

Chapter Three

Trailers: Trailers are much easier for loading or unloading a bike because the ramps are wider and not as steep as a truck bed, plus the ramps are built in to the trailer. The downside, if there is one, is that if you've never driven a trailer before it can be somewhat intimidating. Before heading out into heavy traffic, find a quiet road or large parking lot to practice in. Learn where the blind spots are in your mirrors. You'll probably need to adjust your mirrors a bit farther out in order to see the end of the trailer. Practice making turns because you'll need to swing a little wider to accommodate the trailer behind you. Backing up is the hardest part, but once you've done it a few times and understand the dyslexia involved you'll be fine, but be sure to practice, practice, and practice some more before going out on a busy public roadway.

A "been-there-done-that" note: if you arrive at your destination early and the parking lot is fairly empty, turn the trailer around when you arrive if possible. The parking lot will continue to fill up as the day goes on, and it's much more difficult (and dangerous) to maneuver a trailer in a crowded parking lot, especially if you don't have much experience.

Hitch haulers: The hitch hauler bridges the gap between pickup trucks and trailers. The hauler has several advantages:

- fairly inexpensive
- in most cases lightweight enough for one person to handle
- leaves the truck bed open for coolers and gear
- doesn't require DMV registration as trailers normally do
- is low to the ground for easy loading

When doing your research, the two options for hitch haulers are the ramp style and bottle-jack style. Each has its fan following and it's up to you to decide which will work best for your situation. You'll probably need a Class II hitch or better no matter which style you choose, so check your hitch rating before you buy a hauler. The only downside to the hauler would be if you forget the it's there and back into something. It's easy to remember the hauler when the bike is loaded, but just as easy to forget once the bike is unloaded and you run into town for more snacks.

Whichever mode of transportation you choose, the bike will need to be properly secured.

Securing the Bike for Transport

Once you have the bike loaded into the truck, trailer, or hauler, you'll need to secure it using tie-down straps. Tie-downs with soft straps work best as they do less damage than attaching a metal hook to a metal handlebar (the soft strap goes around the handlebar and the metal S hook attaches to the end of the strap instead of the handlebar). Attach the straps to the handlebars, being careful not to crush any wiring. As you tighten the straps, be sure to pull evenly on both sides so the bike stays straight and does not tilt to one side or the other.

When the bike is secured to your satisfaction, wrap the excess tie-down material around the taut part of the tie-down and secure it in a loose knot so it's not flapping in the breeze. Wind can shred almost anything if it's not secured, and the tie-down could also work its way loose if left flailing.

If you're loading the bike alone and the bike doesn't have a kickstand, put the tie-down straps in place before loading the bike.

It's the driver's responsibility to secure the cargo—don't leave it up to your thirteen-year-old. After travelling a few miles, find a place to stop and check that the tie-downs are still tight, and if you're towing a trailer check the trailer hookup. Before entering a high speed road, make it a point to check the bike and trailer prior to getting on the highway. Any time you make a stop for coffee, or to stretch your legs, always check the bike, trailer, and tie-downs. Another good habit to get into when transporting your bike is to turn the fuel petcock to the "off" position. Just be sure to turn it back to the "on" position before trying to start the bike (another been there, done that).

Security

Thieves love dirt bikes. Most bikes weigh in at around 250 pounds, which two men can easily lift off a trailer or out of a pickup bed. Most States do not require off-road bikes to be registered, inspected, or insured, and they're normally ridden in the woods where police don't patrol. Even if the bike does have a key, the ignition systems are easy to bypass, leaving the thieves a convenient and dependable kick starter. Dirt bikes have few distinguishing features, and even if they did, it's very cheap and easy to install new plastic, so the best advice is: don't let your bike get stolen in the first place.

Thieves are opportunists and will go after the easiest target, so whenever you take your bike out, try to think like a thief:

- don't leave the bike unattended
- always try to park in a well-lit area
- when stopping at the diner, park the truck or trailer where you can see it while eating if possible
- chain the front wheel to the trailer or cable it to the tie-down anchors of the truck bed
- invest in a good trailer hitch lock

It's a good idea to be familiar with the location of the bike's VIN (vehicle identification number), so if it ever does get stolen, you can relay this information to the police. You'll have this information in the paperwork the dealer gave you when you purchased the bike, but if you bought the bike used, take plenty of pictures when you first bring the bike home, and either get an etching of the VIN, or get a good clear photo. The more information you can give to the police, the better your chances are for getting the bike back.

We've discussed many of the practical aspects of owning a dirt bike, such as safety gear, having a safe and legal riding area, transporting the bike, and getting along with your neighbors. You're probably anxious to get to the chapter on buying a bike, but there is one more chapter we need to get through before discussing the bikes. It's a short, but important chapter about excessive noise.

Chapter Four:

Noise

Did you know the word "noise" is derived from the Latin word for "nausea"?

The introduction of the four stroke engine, a huge step forward in most respects, also threatens the sport of dirt bikes like never before due to the increase in noise levels. While excessive noise is not the only factor threatening the future of off-road riding (population explosion, and loss of recreational land also contribute), it is one of the easiest negatives for anti-dirt bikers to point a finger at.

What exactly is excessive noise? Ask any ten people to define excessive noise and you'll probably get ten different answers. One thing is certain though—if your neighbor says your dirt bike is noisy; it's noisy and you'll need to address the issue. We broached the noise versus neighbor subject in Chapter Three, but it warrants further discussion because understanding basic concepts about sound and noise is important for anyone bringing a dirt bike into their residential neighborhood.

The Basics of Sound

The material that sound waves travel through is called the medium (air, water, etc.), and sound waves vary in length according to their frequency. Depending on the source of the sound and the medium it travels through sound can travel long distances very quickly, especially if there is nothing to absorb or deflect the sound waves.

A home theater speaker system is a good way to demonstrate the basics of sound. The placement of the three front speakers, which carry the bulk of the higher frequency dialog and soundtrack, is fairly critical (equidistance to listener, consistent height of the speakers, etc.). Placement of the two surround sound speakers, which carry a wider range of ambient sounds like thunder and gunshots is still important, but has more placement leeway than the front speakers due to the combined medium (read: lower) frequency sounds. The sub-woofer, which delivers the bass sounds, is the least critical speaker to position due to the omni-directional nature of bass (lowest frequency) sounds.

Sound and Dirt Bikes

We haven't discussed the various bike types yet, but there are two engines: the two stroke and the four stroke. Twenty years ago, the two stroke reigned, but now the four stroke has moved to the front row, center stage. Although this move was inevitable, and in most ways welcome, the one drawback has been an increase in noise levels due to the lower frequency sound level of the four stroke engine.

We can loosely apply the home theater example when looking at the noise emitted from dirt bikes. The noise from a two stroke and a four stroke differs in frequency, with the two stroke generating a higher frequency (front speaker) sound and the four stroke generating a lower frequency (sub-woofer) sound. The two stroke may sound louder when you're near the bikes, but the four stroke noise will travel farther and in more directions, potentially annoying more neighbors and bystanders.

Another example of sound-carrying characteristics would be if an eight-year-old and his father were in the backyard and wanted to get Mom's attention, whose voice would travel farther, the high-pitched eight-year-old or the low-pitched forty-year-old? In close proximity the eight-year-old might compete with his Dad, but once the distance increases, Junior won't be heard unless he yells at the top of his lungs (similar to piping an exhaust).

Steps to Keeping the Peace

Sound is a form of energy and won't simply disappear. It needs to dissipate or be converted into another form of energy or matter in order to diminish its energy. If riding on your property is your only option, there are several steps you can take to keep peace in your neighborhood.

Sound can either be reflected or absorbed. Materials that absorb sound are carpets and draperies, which are not practical options in an outdoor environ. Sound engineers say the best weapon against outdoor noise is mass, such as a solid fence or concrete barrier. Obviously a concrete barrier does not lend itself well to most residential areas, but a fence or a dirt berm should be an acceptable alternative. A berm can do double duty by providing a noise barrier as well as a planting base for trees and shrubs. The foliage from trees and shrubs will help in several ways: it provides an "out of sight, out of mind" solution, is pleasant to look at, and also helps reflect and absorb some of the noise. The higher frequency two stroke noise is deflected easier (due to its shorter wavelength) than the lower frequency four stroke, but every little bit helps.

Ironically, a small backyard track calls for a bike that is light, nimble, and able to handle the jumps and constant turns. Motocross bikes lend themselves well to this terrain, but motocross bikes also generate the most noise, making them least suited for close personal contact with neighbors. If you have your heart set on a motocross bike, be sure to look into implementing sound barriers on your property and installing a quieter pipe on your bike. Fortunately, bike manufacturers have come to realize how critical the noise issue is to the future of the sport and have gone to great lengths to make their bikes quieter. Even the aftermarket pipe suppliers have made great strides towards producing quieter products. Do some research and be proactive. It will pay off in the long run.

Chapter Four

If your neighbors are dead set against having dirt bikes in their neighborhood, there may be little that can be done. Most people however, are usually willing to reach a truce if they see you are trying to mitigate the impact your bike will have on the community. Noise is a stimulus, and when people have little control over the source, it can cause stress and anxiety. Include your neighbors in the solution process and try not to trivialize their concerns. Get someone to ride the bikes while you stand in your neighbor's yard. Your helmet can muffle the sound of the bikes and you may not realize how noisy they really are.

You may even find that your neighbors are not upset about the noise at all; they're more afraid the neighborhood is going to be overrun by the Hell's Angels. Communication is the key to a productive, happy, and harmonious relationship.

Chapter Five:

Which Bike?

"I may not have gone where I intended to go, but I think I have ended up where I needed to be." Douglas Adams

Now that you've looked into safety gear, and have taken into account all the details such as having a safe and legal place to ride, excessive noise, and transporting the bike, it's time to start focusing on which bike to buy. There are a lot of model choices and this chapter is meant to help you formulate a list of questions in order to narrow down those choices.

Finding the ideal bike can be difficult, especially for a beginner. You will probably outgrow the first bike you buy, but buying a bike that's too big or too powerful can spell disaster. For new riders, a bike that's too small is definitely better than one that's too big. For those who rode dirt bikes twenty years ago and are just getting back into the sport, you'll be surprised how much the bikes have changed.

Start Small

Let's compare dirt bikes to cell phones. A decade ago, cell phones were big, heavy, cumbersome, and had limited range. Today's cell phones are smaller, lighter, multi-functional and powerful. It's similar with dirt bikes: today's bikes are lighter, sleeker, more nimble and super fast. Most adults on the other hand are heavier, bulkier, and slower than we were twenty years ago. Pair a fast bike with a rusty adult and it could be an accident waiting to happen—trying to raft a Grander Canyon than your abilities allow is just asking for trouble and pain. Even though you'll lose some money on depreciation, your health and well-being are priceless. Buy a bike that's within your ability and trade up as your level of experience grows. Safety first!!

We'll touch on buying a used bike shortly, but we're going to focus on buying new as opposed to buying used since beginners normally don't have enough experience to determine if a bike is in good mechanical condition. Dealer support is also much more important at the beginner stage. Finally, you know the bike you bought is in good working order so you won't have to worry as much about something breaking, leaving you to focus on your riding.

We're also going to focus on the Big Five bike manufacturers (Honda, Kawasaki, KTM, Suzuki and Yamaha) because of the well established and widespread dealer support these manufacturers offer. Husaberg, Husqvarna, and GasGas all make excellent bikes, but their dealer network is not as extensive. Beginners should stick with mainstream bikes. The exception of course, is if you're interested in a trials bikes (more on this later). Then you'll be looking into dealers that sell Sherco, Beta, Scorpa, and Montesa.

The first step to choosing a bike is to determine what type of riding you'll be doing, and that may be pre-determined in a large part by the availability of riding facilities in your area (i.e., track or trails). You also need to consider your personality. Are you a speed demon? Jump monkey? The slow, steady type? All bikes have different characteristics to match different personalities. The trick is to define which characteristic matches your riding style and personality the closest.

Additional criteria that will influence your decision will be: your budget, dealer proximity, seat height and weight of the bike, decibel levels, whether to buy new or used, and whether to choose a two stroke or four stroke.

Two Stroke vs. Four Stroke

If you used to ride dirt bikes as a kid, chances are it was a two stroke. Starting in the late '90's, four strokes gained a toehold into the dirt bike scene, and have continued to catapult their way to the forefront of the dirt bike world. Many riders find the current crop of four stroke bikes easy to ride with their smooth, tractable power delivery, but not all riders, especially those with some experience, want that predictability. They prefer the thrill and adrenaline rush of hitting the powerband of a snappy two stroke. So what's the difference and which is better?

Two strokes: The two stroke engine involves two processes: compression and combustion. The engine fires and the spark plug ignites once every revolution of the crankshaft. It's a simpler process with fewer moving parts, which makes them easier to work on and lighter in weight than a comparable four stroke. Since it fires on every revolution, it is twice as powerful as a four stroke engine, which is one of the reasons they allow 250cc two strokes to compete with 450cc four strokes on the motocross track. There are die-hard two stroke fans that won't be caught dead on a four stroke, but there are a few characteristics of two strokes that some people may find objectionable:

- the two strokes require a mixture of gas and pre-mix oil, so you need to be sure to have extra oil on hand—you may be able to find someone in the parking lot willing to donate some gasoline, but without the pre-mix oil the gas does you no good
- the two strokes tend to smoke when they're first started up, which may annoy your neighbors
- although the sound is not as loud as a four stroke, some people do not like the higher frequency "buzzing" sound of a two stroke
- they can be difficult to ride due to their unpredictable power delivery

Most two stroke fans will say these objections are outweighed by the positive aspects:

- since there are fewer moving parts, they're less expensive to maintain and easier to work on
- the sound of a two stroke does not travel as far as the sound of a four stroke
- they're lighter, more nimble, and easier to maneuver
- they are an absolute blast to ride due to their unpredictable power delivery

Four strokes: The four stroke engine involves four processes: intake, compression, combustion and exhaust. It fires only once every two revolutions. The power delivery is steady and predictable making them a great choice for beginners or rusty riders, but four stroke bikes have their share of detractors as well:

- they require a bit more maintenance
- motocross four strokes are very loud
- more moving parts can mean more things to break
- they can be hard to start when they get hot
- some riders say they're too easy to ride due to their predictable power delivery

The flip side however, has many positives:

- the gas and oil are separate, which can be an advantage—if you run out of gas, as all you need is a gas can
- some bikes are loud, but they can be modified to bring the sound levels down
- with proper maintenance they will last a long time between major overhauls
- there are many more four stroke models to choose from than two stroke models
- a four stroke is more fuel efficient than a two stroke
- they are great bikes to learn on due to their predictable power delivery

The four stroke bikes are evolving and improving every year. All the Big Five four-stroke bikes (250cc-450cc) are now fuel-injected (Yamaha being the last to jump on board).

To a certain extent, your two-stroke vs. four-stroke decision is a foregone conclusion since three out of the Big Five manufacturers no longer make adult two strokes. KTM and Yamaha are the only ones offering adult-sized two stroke bikes in 2014.

So which is better? The short answer is: neither. They're different bikes built for different purposes and rider personalities. It's like asking which is better: an acoustic guitar or an electric guitar. Both guitars are great instruments made for creating different types of music. They both provide hours of enjoyment, bring people together to relax and socialize, and that's exactly what dirt bikes do. Buy the bike that best suits your abilities For beginners or those who are the least bit apprehensive, absolutely start with a four stroke and work your way up from there.

New or Used?

Used bikes: Those who have some experience with dirt bikes may find it worthwhile to buy a used bike, but keep in mind the nature of dirt bikes is one of constant punishment, especially for motocross bikes. If you find a bike that sounds promising, pepper the seller with plenty of questions and go with your gut instinct. Here is a very basic list of questions you would ask any seller:

- are you the original owner
- do you have a clear title
- has the bike been raced
- who maintained the bike and do you have the maintenance records
- do you have the owner's manual
- why are you selling the bike

You'll need to judge the seller as much as the bike. Take a look at his house and property to see if they are well kept. Chances are his bikes will be in a similar condition.

When looking at used bikes, be very leery about bikes that don't have official paperwork. We touched on security in Chapter Three, and you don't want to end up buying a stolen bike. Check the VIN to be sure it hasn't been filed off or defaced in any way. That would be a dead giveaway that is something is not right. Before heading out to see a used bike, look up the number of the local law enforcement agency. This way if you have any doubts, you can call and ask them to run the VIN number or ask if there are any reports of that year and model bike being stolen. If the seller balks, it should be a red flag that something is not right.

If you're not confident that you have the "horse sense" you need to buy a used bike, be patient and hold out for a new one. In the end, it's Caveat Emptor (let the buyer beware!)

New bikes: Buying a new bike is much easier of course, but there are a few things to keep in mind. Many dealers offer low interest rates known as "teaser rates" for the first few months to entice you to sign on the dotted line, so be sure to ask what the actual finance rate is after the teaser rate expires.

While the Internet offers some enticing deals, it's always best to deal with a local shop when buying new. You may need to bring the bike to the dealer for servicing in order to keep it under warranty, which means you'll have to load the bike and drive to the dealer so the closer the shop is, the less time it will take. Note—most motocross bikes don't come with any warranty at all. Once it's out of the showroom, you're on your own!

The following section delves into more detail about each type of bike along with some of their pros and cons.

Types of Off-Road Bikes

The three main off-road bike types are: dual sport, motocross, and trail. A fourth option is a trials bike, which is an excellent option for folks with very little property or hostile neighbors. Each bike is made for a specific type of riding, and there is no one perfect bike. There are regional differences as well; a trail bike that works well for the tree lined single-track of the northeast may not work as well for the wide open deserts out west. We'll start to narrow down the bike choices by examining the pros and cons of the four bike types.

Dual-sport bikes: A dual-sport bike is a purpose-built street legal trail bike, meaning it can be ridden on-road or off-road. It has a minimum of a headlight, taillight, mirrors, turn signals, horn, and street legal muffler. There are pros and cons to dual-sport bikes as there are with any product that tries to serve two purposes.

Pros:

- convenience and versatility: if you have a trail system nearby, you can hop on the bike and ride to the trails, which is much easier than loading the bikes onto a truck or trailer
- they are fuel efficient and quiet
- they open up more riding opportunities, (i.e., enduro competitions)
- they have a headlight which can extend riding time and make the bike more visible to other riders, upping the safety factor
- large gas tanks mean longer rides without re-fueling
- most dual-sport bikes have electric start

Cons:

- extra weight: most dual-sport bikes are quite a bit heavier than the same size trail bike, so when (remember it's when, not if) you fall, you'll have to lift those extra pounds, and the added weight can also make them difficult to maneuver if you ride on tight trails

- when riding off-road the turn signals and mirrors are very vulnerable to breakage either from falls, or those trees you thought you could squeeze through (low profile turn signals may be a worthwhile investment)
- the suspension is not good for jumping
- you'll need to pay registration and insurance fees just as with a street bike

Can you convert a trail bike to a dual sport bike? Yes and no. It depends on your State's DMV laws. Each State has different equipment requirements for street legal motorcycles, including such items as DOT approved tires, left and right side mirrors, turn signals, horn, headlight, taillight, speedometers, quiet exhaust, chain guards, and side reflectors. A few aftermarket companies sell off-road conversion kits (sometimes called Baja kits), but lights alone won't make a bike street legal. Contact your State's Department of Motor Vehicles for a list of equipment and paperwork that is required for street motorcycles and decide if it's worth the effort and cost.

Motocross bikes: Motocross bikes are happiest when they're leaping, flying, and snarling at the terrain, which makes them the perfect choice if your main riding area is a motocross track. They're also a good fit for small backyard tracks but as we discussed in Chapter Four, motocross bikes are extremely noisy so you'll need to address the noise issue if you have neighbors nearby. The seat height of motocross bikes is quite tall, which can be a problem for beginners and vertically challenged riders. Most motocross bikes do not yet have electric start and the tall seat height can make it difficult to kick start the bike if you can't touch the ground solidly.

Motocross bikes normally aren't equipped with a headlight, kickstand, or spark arrestor, which are all very convenient if you want to hit the trails. The spark arrestor is not only convenient, but is almost assuredly mandatory if you're going to spend time on public trails, especially if the trail system is part of a national forest. Motocross bikes are great fun once you get used to them, but the abrupt power delivery can be a rude awakening for the uninitiated. They can be modified to be better behaved on trails, but you're better off getting a trail bike if trails are your main riding areas.

Pros:

- lightweight
- perfect for motocross tracks
- fun to ride (once you get used to them)
- fits well on small acreage
- purpose built for jumping obstacles

Cons:

- very noisy
- tall seat height for the average sized rider
- no kickstand, headlight, or spark arrestor
- fuel tank is small
- most motocross bikes do not have electric start

Be very careful the first few times you take any motocross bike out on the trails as the bike will handle much differently on the trails than on the track.. You can make a few changes know as mods (modifications) to MX bikes that will make them easier to ride on the trails:

- soften the suspension
- add a flywheel weight
- change the gearing (sprockets)
- change the pipe

Try one modification at a time and keep track of all the changes you make. If you add two or more mods at one time and you're not happy with the results, you won't know which mod is causing the problem.

Trail bikes: If your main riding area is a trail system, your best bet is to buy a bike specifically made for that purpose. Trail bikes are quiet, and the four strokes are very easy to ride. Most come equipped with a headlight, taillight, quiet exhaust, kickstand and spark arrestor. The suspension is comfortable and geared towards longer trail rides as opposed to quick laps around the track. The gas tank is larger than the tanks on motocross bikes to allow for longer rides since you'll be much farther away from the parking area where your gas can is stored. The radiator is also larger to keep the bike cool when riding at a slower pace. And finally, they have a wider gear ratio which means you won't have to shift every milli-second. Electric start is pretty much standard on most trail bikes.

Some of the higher performance trail bikes (especially the KTMs) can be ridden on a motocross track, but don't expect to keep up with your buddies who ride motocross bikes, or expect to be able to jump huge obstacles. You'll also want to check with the track officials to find out if you need to tape over the headlight and/or remove the kickstand.

Pros:

- quiet
- smooth power delivery (four strokes)
- most trail bikes have a headlight, kickstand and spark arrestor
- electric start
- larger fuel tank than motocross bikes

Cons:

- heavier than motocross bikes
- not ideal for jumping large jumps

Trials bikes: No, that's not a typo. It's a trials bike as opposed to a trail bike. These lightweight and quiet bikes are made for riding through a rugged obstacle course. They are ridden at a very slow pace and the object is for the rider to complete the course without losing his or her balance and touching the ground with any part of their body. They are not as mainstream as the other bikes, and they're not the best choice for long trail rides, but for folks with very little property, rugged terrain, or hostile noise-hating neighbors, these bikes are the perfect choice.

Some of the best Endurocross riders (David Knight and Taddy Blazusiak come to mind) got their start riding trials bikes. Trials bikes have been hugely popular in Europe for decades and the U.S. is catching on quickly. There's a Trial Training Center which is a 650 acre resort located in Sequatchie, Tennessee that offers training packages as well as hosting trials competitions.

Pros:

- perfect for small or rocky acreage
- sewing-machine quiet
- lightweight
- easy to learn on

Cons:

- there is no seat
- purpose built (not made to be trail ridden)
- dealer network is not as extensive as mainstream bikes

Electric bikes: They don't fit into any one particular category, but electric dirt bikes will definitely be a big part of the off-road landscape in the near future, so they bear mention. As with any beta version, they have a long way to go before they're accepted as mainstream, but the seed of possibility has been planted especially since KTM has committed its vast resources to the Freeride E electric bike. The other e-bike holding its own for several years is the Zero FX from Zero manufacturing.

In some ways it's sad to see the electric bikes take over because there's just something about the roar of a dirt bike and the smell of burnt fuel that is so much a part of the sport, but times change and we need to change with them. Better electric than not at all.

A List of Questions

Any purchase comes with questions, whether you're buying a house (is the neighborhood friendly? how long is my commute? what services are nearby?) or a garbage can (how many gallons? is the lid raccoon-proof? should I buy one with wheels?), and purchasing a dirt bike is no exception.

The following is a list of questions to ask yourself when deciding to buy a dirt bike. Two of the most important questions pertain to safety equipment and having a place to ride. Many of the questions can be applied to both new and used bikes, but the list is geared towards buying new. It also gets more complicated for those with families. Make sure you spouse/significant other is okay with this.

- why am I buying a bike

- do I have the necessary safety equipment
- where will I ride the bike
- do I want to ride motocross or trails
- how noisy is the bike
- can I afford it
- what will the payment be
- which dealer is closest
- what happens if I get hurt
- how will I transport the bike
- how much does the bike weigh
- where will I store and secure it
- what's the seat height
- do I want a two-stroke or four-stroke

No One-Size-Fits-All

There is no one perfect bike that can fit all riding disciplines. Choose your main riding style and riding area, then buy the bike that best suits that type of riding.

Now that you have an idea which bike type might work best, it's time to do some in-depth research in order to narrow down the choices even more. While doing your research, you will come across the ciphered manufacturer's model information. The next chapter will help explain what the letters and numbers mean, as well as offer a few more tips to help narrow down your bike choice.

Chapter Six:
Narrowing Your Choices

"You know you're in love when you can't fall asleep because reality is finally better than your dreams."
Dr. Seuss

By now you should have some idea of which bike will work best for you based on available riding areas, your personality, and your finances. Compile a wish list of all the bikes that meet your criteria then continue with your research. Finding objective information isn't easy, so keep searching and take the time to sift through all the pluses and minuses of each bike.

Start Doing Your Research

Go to the manufacturer's websites and read up on the different models on your list. Keep in mind that the manufacturers want you to buy their bikes, so they go through great pains to make them sound like the perfect bike for everyone. In other words—you need to sift through some of the hype and propaganda. Be sure to read their summaries with a keen eye and open mind. Try to find time to visit some dealers in order to get an idea of the physical aspects of each bike, especially the seat height and weight.

Dirt bike magazines are another great source of information. Most issues have some type of bike comparisons (called shootouts) that detail the pros and cons of each bike. Visit the magazine's website and you'll probably find archived articles on past shootouts. Dirt Rider has been around for a long, long, time and is a great resource. They have a great YouTube channel as well. There is also Transworld Motocross, and Motocross Action magazine.

Join Internet forums if you haven't already, and ask questions about the bikes you like, but be sure to post your height, weight, and riding ability. If you don't give enough information, someone may respond that a CRF 450R is a great bike, which is true, but it's not a great bike for a beginner. Try searching for regional forums because they have the advantage of being able to explain which bike is best for the differences in the local terrain. Once they get to know you and feel comfortable, they may even invite you out to their riding area and let you try out their bike, which is the best way to find out if the bike is a good fit for you.

A note about bike weight—most manufacturers advertise their bike's weight in a "ready to ride" condition, meaning the advertised weight includes all the fluids (brake, tranny, fuel) with a gas tank that's 90% full. Only KTM lists their bike weights without fuel, so if you're looking at a KTM, you'll need to multiply the size of the gas tank by the weight of the gasoline (gasoline weighs a little over six pounds per gallon) in order to get a more accurate picture.

The next step to narrowing your bike choice is to get each bike's specifications from the manufacturer's website. *Figure 1-1* shows the specifications for a 2014 Honda CRF 250R motocross bike. For most beginners, items such as bore, stroke, and induction won't be as important as seat height, weight, and the capacity of the gas tank. *Figure 1-2* shows close-up details of some of the specifications for the same bike. Go to the websites for each bike you're interested in and look through the bike's specifications so you can compare apples to apples.

Figure 1-1 2014 Honda CRF 250R specifications

Figure 1-2 2014 Honda CRF 250R specs detail

	adjustability, 12.2 inches travel
Rear Suspension	Pro-Link® Showa® single shock v adjustability, and compression-d: high-speed (3.5 turns); 12.3 inch
Front Brake	Single 240mm disc with twin-pis
Rear Brake	Single 240mm disc
Front Tire	Dunlop MX51FA 80/100-21
Rear Tire	Dunlop MX51 100/90-19

DIMENSIONS

Rake	27° 23' (Caster Angle)
Trail	118mm (4.6 inches)
Wheelbase	58.6 inches
Seat Height	37.4 inches
Curb Weight	231 pounds (includes all standa
Fuel Capacity	1.66 gallons
Ground Clearance	12.7 inches

OTHER

Available Color	Red
Model ID	CRF250R

When comparing the different models, a suggestion would be to print the specifications for every bike you're interested in, then use different color highlighters and highlight each component (i.e., seat height, weight, etc.) you like or dislike with a different color marker. Highlight everything you like in green, everything you don't like in red (or pink), and everything you're not sure about in yellow. When you're done, the spec sheets will give you a good idea of which bike might work best based on the amount of green, yellow, or red highlights.

Although the spec sheets are a good place to start, they don't tell you everything about the bike. Researching Yamaha's trail bike, the 2013 WR 250F, you would need to look under the "features" tab to find out that it has electric start and a headlight and taillight because that information isn't listed under "specifications". With Honda's trail bike, the 2013 CRF 250X, although they list the electric start in the specifications, you would need to click on the "360 degree spin" to see that it sports a headlight and taillight. These components aren't listed in the specs or the brochure (which is a surprise), so click through all the tabs to get the complete details.

Once the basics have been compared on paper, do a general Internet search for each model to get more opinions. Try "2014 Honda CRF 250X opinions" or "2014 Suzuki RM-Z 250 reviews". Most of the reviews and opinions will be written by experienced riders, but they still offer insight to the bike's characteristics. Now it's time to get some real-life feedback from friends, club members, forum users, and even the dealer. Collect as many pieces of information as possible, then start putting together the puzzle.

> In 1974 you could walk out the door with a Honda CR125 Elsinore for under $800. A 2014 Yamaha YZ125 lists for $6290. How's that for inflation?

De-Coding the Code

Dirt bikes aren't given names like cars or ATVs; they're given numbers and initials (i.e. YZ 250F). The initials tell you the manufacturers' model, the number is the engine's cubic centimeter displacement, and any other initials denote additional bike characteristics. When researching bikes, be sure you're comparing oranges to oranges. Also be aware that the manufacturers sometimes change model names (for example, in 2006 KTM changed the EXC model line to the XCW model line).

We'll take a look at the Honda CRF 150F as an example. The CRF tells you it's a Honda four stroke dirt bike, model CRF. The two strokes were called CRs, but Honda doesn't make two strokes anymore, so there is just the CRF, no matter how big or small the bike is. The number 150 refers to the engine displacement of 150 cubic centimeters (actually 149, but that's not relevant at present). The F at the end of the 150 is Honda's model designation. Compare that to the CRF 150R which is a full-on motocross race bike, and the CRF 150RB, which is a full-on motocross race bike with bigger wheels. Honda's website has the 150F listed under "off-road" and the 150R is listed under "motocross". Most websites will have the bikes listed by category, which helps figure out which bike is a trail bike and which is a motocross bike. KTM lists their trail bikes under "Enduro" while all others list them under "off-road".

Each manufacturer has its own letter/number combinations. While Honda uses CRF 250R to designate a four stroke motocross bike, Kawasaki uses KX 250F, preferring to put the "F" (four stroke) designation after the number. It may sound confusing, but once you've read a few of the summaries on the websites it should be easier to understand. You can also assign your own code to make the many different models easier to categorize. Using the Honda 150F and 150R example again, the "F" can stand for "fun bike" and the "R" can stand for "race bike".

An Overview of Bike Models

Bikes models come and go, but a few remain the same year after year. The following list shows some of the bikes that make up the backbone of the industry, and should help determine which bike belongs in which category (dual-sport, trail, motocross, etc.). Most average sized adult males will need a full-sized bike, not because of the power, but for the ergonomics, so the smaller trail bikes are listed at the end of the next chapter (Chapter Seven).

As mentioned, models come and go. It appears Honda does not have the long running 250X trail bike listed in their 2014 lineup and Yamaha doesn't show the WR 250F. Both bikes have been around for years and nobody except the manufacturers know if they will be added to the lineup again, but since they've been around for so long, they're being included in the list. Both bikes are available in 2013 models.

Dual-Sport Bikes: (all are four strokes)

Since this book is aimed at beginners, the bikes on this list are 650ccs and under, which have more than enough power. The adventure bikes go up to 1200 ccs, but they're for experienced riders only.

200 - 250cc	Honda CRF 250L
	Kawasaki KLX 250S
	Suzuki DR 200SE
	Yamaha TW 200, XT 250 and WR 250R

350 - 450cc	KTM 350 EXC-F
	Suzuki DR-Z 400S and 400SM

500 - 690cc	KTM 500 EXC-F
	BMW-F 650GS
	Honda XR 650L
	Kawasaki KLR 650
	Suzuki V-Strom 650 and DR 650
	KTM 690 Enduro R

Motocross bikes:

125cc (two stroke)	KTM 125 SX
	Yamaha YZ 125

150cc (two stroke)	KTM 150 SX

250cc (two stroke)	KTM 250 SX
	Yamaha YZ 250

250cc (four	Honda CRF 250R
	Kawasaki KX 250F

stroke) KTM 250 SX-F
Suzuki RM-Z 250
Yamaha YZ 250F

350-   Honda CRF 450R
450cc   Kawasaki KX 450F
(four   KTM 350 SX-F
stroke) KTM 450 SX-F
Suzuki RM-Z 450
Yamaha YZF 450

Trail bikes:

150-   KTM 150 XC
200cc   KTM 200 XC-W
(two
stroke)

230cc   Honda CRF 230
(four   Yamaha TT-R 230
Stroke)

250cc   KTM 250 XC
(two   KTM 250 XC-W
stroke)

250cc   Honda CRF 250X
(four   KTM 250 XCF
stroke) KTM 250 XCF-W
Yamaha WR 250F

300cc   KTM 300 XC

(two stroke)	KTM 300 XC-W
350cc (four stroke)	KTM 350 XC-F KTM 350XCF-W
450-500cc (four stoke)	Honda CRF 450X Kawasaki KLX 450R KTM 450 XC-F KTM 450 XC-W KTM 500 XC-W Yamaha WR 450F

Trials Bikes:

125cc	Beta EVO 125 GasGas TXT Pro 125 Scorpa SR 125
250cc	Beta EVO 250 GasGas TXT Pro 250
280cc	GasGas TXT Pro 280 Scorpa SR 280
300cc	Beta EVO 300 GasGas TXT Pro 300 Sherco 2.9 Access

Down To the Wire

By now you should have narrowed your choices to three or four bikes. If you haven't been to a dealer yet, go look at the bikes in person but check the manufacturer's website first. You can save a significant amount of money with rebates, especially on leftover models. Check for financing offers, (but don't forget the "teaser rate" warning earlier). Cash is still king with used bikes, and still matters with new bikes, but not to the same extent, although it can't hurt to have a pocketful of money if you can afford it. Test ride the bike if you're ready, but don't be in a rush. After months of looking at pictures and poring over specs sheets, it's very easy to get caught up in the excitement of actually getting on a bike and hearing the engine roar to life.

Most dealers are trustworthy, reliable, and want to retain you as a loyal customer, but their goal is to sell bikes so it's up to you to be an informed consumer. Test ride the bikes, hear the differences in the noise levels, and muscle them around the parking lot (especially the ladies). Remember, you'll have to load and unload the bike onto a truck, trailer or hauler, plus you'll be picking it up when you fall. Keep in mind the trails are not as smooth and wide open as the dealer's parking lot, so if you're struggling with the bike in the lot, it will be many times worse out on the trails.

When you finally decide which bike you want, try to make a deal. See if the dealer will price match another manufacturer's offer. Be creative when bargaining—just because the dealer won't lower the price doesn't mean you can't ask for a free maintenance contract or some free riding gear. Once you've bought the bike, ask the dealer to set up the suspension for your weight, especially if you're not the average weight for the bike's target market. Ask him to make sure the ergonomics work for your body's frame. He can raise or lower the bars, and move the clutch and/or brake levers if need be. Taller riders can purchase a taller seat, and if you're a shorter rider, you can ask how to go about shaving the seat if he can't get the bike low enough through re-setting the suspension (it's doubtful he'll be willing to shave the seat on a brand new bike so you'll probably have to do this on your own later on).

Don't make any changes to the bike yourself unless you're sure you know what you are doing. Have the dealer do it for you the first time and ask him to explain the process so you can make adjustments to the bike as your riding and mechanical aptitude improves.

On the flip side, if you're not sure which bike is for you, walk away. Now that you have more information from your visit to the dealer, return to the Internet and ask for opinions about the bike on discussion forums. Tell other forum users what you liked and did not like about the bike. If you're a member of a club, talk to some of the other members. Try to find out if anyone else has the same bike. If not, there's probably a reason why they've shied away from that model. Read the magazine articles again, and go back to the manufacturer's websites. Continue to compare the pros and cons of each bike, and repeat the process as many times as necessary.

Unfortunately, there is no one-size-fits-all magic formula for choosing a dirt bike. Height, weight, age, fitness, personality, access to riding areas, and finances all contribute to the final decision. Ultimately only you can make that decision. It's a big decision to make, so do your homework and take your time deciding.

We've covered much of the criteria for selecting the right bike, but women have fewer options and face more hurdles when buying a dirt bike, so the following chapter addresses some of the obstacles women face when deciding which bike is best.

Chapter Seven:
A Few Words for the Ladies

"Nobody really cares if you're miserable, so you might as well be happy." Cynthia Nelms

Riding dirt bikes may be a male-dominated sport, but there is no reason for women not to join their friends and family out on the trails. Yes, riding dirt bikes can be dangerous, dirty, and intimidating, but you can still join in the fun on your own terms and at your own pace.

We'll start this chapter with a few questions and answers.

Questions and Answers

Q: Will I fall?

A: Yes. Absolutely, unequivocally, and beyond a doubt. Riding dirt bikes, just like any other active sport, has a certain element of danger, and accidents will happen. There is no getting around the fact that you're going to fall now and again, so if that scares you, riding dirt bikes may not be the sport for you.

Q: Do they make riding gear for women?

A: Yes. There is quite a good selection of riding and safety gear made specifically for women. Chapter Twelve lists a few online stores. Visit several sites for the most complete selection and best price.

Q: What if I've never ridden before?

A: We covered this in Chapter Two, but it bears repeating. Anyone who has never ridden a motorcycle of any kind, street or dirt, should take the Motorcycle Safety Foundation Basic Rider Course or Dirt Bike Course. This will tell you whether or not riding a bike is something you might enjoy. If you're scared in the class riding around on smooth blacktop, you'll know dirt bikes aren't for you. For those who have ridden street bikes but not dirt bikes, be aware of the differences in weight, seat height and ergonomics between the two. Find out if there are any off-road parks near you. Ask if they rent bikes and if they have anyone willing to help you get started in a quiet out of the way area.

Q: I'm only 5'1"— am I too short?

A: Not at all, but you'll be limited to a smaller selection of bikes, at least until you gain some experience and confidence.

Q: Will I need to use a clutch?

A: Yes. The only bikes that have auto-clutches are those made for small children.

Q: What if I don't have anyone to ride with?

A: Don't ride by yourself! You could get lost, hurt, or stranded. That doesn't apply only to women, but to all riders. Try contacting some of the area clubs or post in some of your local area forums. There may be other women in a similar situation that would love to have a riding friend. Male friends can be good riding buddies, but keep it to one or two, especially if you're a new rider. Once they get in a group, guys can get caught up in the pack mentality and may leave you stranded for a while if you can't keep up.

Some Kinder, Gentler Advice

The bike manufacturers build bikes with their primary consumer in mind (men), but there are still plenty of bike choices for women, and as you gain experience you'll have even more bikes to choose from. Chapters Five and Six laid out a plan for choosing a bike based on the type of riding you will be doing and the same criteria applies to women, but there are a few other things women need to bear in mind when choosing a bike.

Seat height and electric start: Seat height is one of the biggest safety considerations for beginner riders, and is especially important for women, who are typically shorter than men. If you're not able to touch the ground, the bike will tip over every time you come to a stop and what goes down must come up, leading to more time spent picking the bike up than riding it. That's dangerous, embarrassing, physically exhausting and definitely not fun. The fear factor will creep in, eroding your confidence. Buy a bike with a low enough seat height that you're able to touch the ground, at least with the balls of your feet. It's even more crucial for you to be able to touch the ground if the bike does not have electric start.

Weight: The weight of the bike is another important factor. Men are taller (more leverage) and have more muscle mass (strength), so picking up a 250 pound bike is less of a struggle for men than it is for women. Check the weight of the bike that you're interested in. Don't assume that a smaller bike weighs less than its big brother. Entry level fun bikes aren't normally built with high-end components. They're meant to be casual trail bikes, not race bikes where light weight is very important. The weight will also come into play when loading and unloading the bike on a truck or trailer because the bike will need to be pushed up onto the truck or trailer. When test riding a bike, try pushing it around the parking lot after you're done riding to get a feel for how heavy it is.

Motocross bikes: Motocross is a very aggressive sport. It's fast, furious and sometimes unforgiving, but also loads of fun if you've got the wherewithal to run with the pack. It's definitely not for the faint of heart or thin of skin. You won't find any princesses there. It probably comes as no surprise that guys are aggressive riders, which can make the motocross track even more intimidating. Visit the track a few times and decide if motocross might be a possibility.

A big drawback for women wanting to ride a motocross bike is the tall seat height, and most motocross bikes do not have electric starters yet, which makes the tall seat height even more of a problem. The other drawback (for beginners) is the snappy power delivery, even with a four stroke. These bikes are made to accelerate for short bursts around an obstacle-filled track. For riders with some experience, this won't be much of a problem, but if you have no experience at all it can be intimidating and perhaps dangerous. You should steer clear of motocross bikes when first starting out.

Go With Your Intuition

You're the kinder, gentler, more level-headed gender and you were given intuition for a reason. Go with your gut instinct. If you think a bike is too tall or too powerful and you don't feel comfortable, don't let anyone tell you that "you'll grow into it". Yes, you may lose money if you outgrow the smaller bike, but money means nothing when it comes to your safety. If you're scared all the time, you won't ride well or you won't ride at all, and you'll end up selling the bike for a loss anyway. Stay the course and buy the bike that you feel suits you best.

It's your responsibility to do your own research. Try to get as much objective information as possible before going to the dealer. This might not be easy so don't get discouraged. Take your time and don't fall for the hard sell. Take the information the dealer has given you and evaluate it. They may be giving you a great deal, but it may be a great deal on the wrong bike.

Final Thoughts

- don't let anyone tell you a two stroke is better—they're great bikes, but a two stroke is not a good beginner bike
- be sure you can touch the ground, at least with the balls of your feet
- don't let anyone tell you you'll grow into the bike
- you shouldn't ride by yourself, but if the guys (or gals) you end up riding with are more experienced, don't try to keep up—if they have to wait for you at every intersection, too bad
- if the bike you're looking at does not have electric start, kick start the bike yourself
- don't let the dealer kick start the bike for you—you may think he's being a nice guy (which may be true), but you need to find out for yourself how difficult kick starting a

> bike can be especially if you can't reach the ground comfortably
> * don't let anyone make you feel stupid or guilty— take as much time as you need to make an intelligent decision when buying or riding your bike

The smaller dual-sport bikes listed in Chapter Six will fit most women, but here's a list of smaller off-road beginner trail and motocross bikes:

Trail bikes:

* Honda CRF 125F
* Honda CRF 150F
* Kawasaki KLX 140
* Suzuki DR-Z 125L
* Yamaha TTR 125 LE

Motocross bikes:

* Honda CRF 150R (four stroke)
* Kawasaki KX100 (two stroke)

Chapter Eight:
Clubs Are Essential

"The secret to getting ahead is getting started."
Sally Berger

Riding dirt bikes, like most sports, is a social activity. Sure, you can ride alone now and again but it's much more fun riding with friends and family. If none of your friends or family have bikes, the best way to find new people to ride with is to join a club in your area. This may be easier said than done as there may not be any off-road clubs near your neighborhood.

Location, Location, Location

Your geographic location has a lot to do with the available riding opportunities. There are several million acres of public land throughout the United States, but the distribution of that land is very unbalanced, with the bulk of the open land being out West. Much of the open space on the East Coast is either privately owned, suffocated with houses and commercial development, or already being used as a recreation area. The opposite is true for the land out West, where it is much more difficult to develop the land for year-round human habitation (think desert).

What if there are no existing clubs for you to join? It's a daunting project, but why not consider starting a club of your own?

Starting Your Own Club

A club can offer many benefits such as:

- speaking with one voice for a larger group which increases your clout with elected officials (read: more votes)
- offering a single point of contact which may make property owners more comfortable allowing access to their land

- promoting responsible behavior and safety through education and social interaction, which will help improve the image of off-road riders to the general public
- providing a great social network of like-minded enthusiasts
- lowering costs via sharing expenses (car pooling, trailer sharing, gear trades)

It will be difficult to get people to join an off-road club unless there is access to a riding area or at least some organized riding events, so the first thing a fledgling club needs to do is to secure a place to ride, preferably less than two hours away. If there is no legal place to ride, look closely at the land in your town and see if you can find any large unused properties (old dumps, unused quarries, etc). Ask the town assessor if he or she knows of any properties that might be suitable for an off-road park. If you find a parcel of land on your own that you're curious about, call (or better yet, stop by) the town assessor's office to find out who owns the property. You'll need to get used to making cold calls. It doesn't hurt to ask and the worst they can say is "no".

If there is no available town property, look into any State land in the area. Find out the trail designations and allowed users. Visit the area to get an idea if it will work for dirt bikes. Does it have an adequate parking and unloading area? Is it large enough to allow a separate area for off-road riders? If not, how can off-road riding be integrated with other recreational users? Do your research before calling the governing agency. Anticipate questions or reservations, and formulate as many answers as possible ahead of time.

Advice for Getting Started

First steps: Incorporating your club is a good idea right from the start. It adds a level of professionalism and insulates the club's officers from personal liability. Each State has different laws, so you'll need to do a search for "non-profit incorporation (your state)". Although most new clubs will be operating on a shoestring, it would behoove you to find the funds to consult a lawyer or accountant to help set up the corporation. Most attorneys will lower their fees once they see you are a non-profit.

When choosing a name for your club, try to steer clear of the "bad boy" names like *dirt demons*, *rutbusters*, or even *trail blazers*. Try to think of a more generic name that doesn't lead people to think you're going out there to rip the trails to shreds. It would also be smart to check that the domain name is available. Domains run about $10-$15 per year and it's a good idea to have it for the future. You can always let it expire if you decide you don't need it.

Realistic expectations: Keep in mind that ten percent of the members will end up doing ninety percent of the work, so keep your expectations realistic. Many potential members are only interested in the short term goal of having a place to ride and have no intention of going to meetings, participating in work days, or putting anything back into the club.

Many clubs (not just off-road clubs) require their members to perform workdays a few times per year. This is a great way to get members to invest in the club. Be flexible though—if a member's wife is due to give birth, you don't want to drag him out to the middle of the woods where there may not be a cell phone signal. At the same time, decide how many times you'll allow a member to use the old "but my kid has a baseball game" excuse.

A quick aside—for those who think that opening an off-road park is an impossible task, consider the following story about patience and persistence. Long Island, New York is one of the most densely populated places in the United States, and due to its proximity to New York City, the real estate prices border on obscene. The island is only 118 miles long by 23 miles wide, but somehow a few dedicated individuals have managed to get a recreational trail facility opened (the Long Island Recreational Trails Conservancy).

This should serve as a benchmark for anyone thinking that getting an off-road area opened can't be done. Visit their website (www. lirtc.org) and you will see an excellent example of how to create a family friendly, community based riding area. Starting a club will be hard work, but the only failure in life is not trying.

It ain't gonna be easy: Organizing an off-road club will be a difficult project no matter where you live, but the folks out West, where some eighty percent of the land is in the public domain, will find more land (and public support) for a trail system or off-road riding area than someone living on the East Coast in a smaller state like Rhode Island or Connecticut. Those in the northeast will need plenty of that Yankee tenacity coupled with a strong commitment and a healthy dose of pure luck. Chapter Twelve has links to several organizations that offer help and support to new clubs across the country.

Embarking on a quest to start an off-road club or gain access to a piece of land can be overwhelming. Here are a few things to keep in mind:

- develop goals and strategies: put your plan down on paper to help keep you focused, productive, and efficient
- follow up: there's a fine line between being persistent and being annoying, so try hard to figure out where that line is and don't cross it
- be professional: "when in Rome, do as the Romans do" is a valuable piece of advice—be yourself, but take some cues from the people around you as far as mannerisms, speech, and dress code
- create some type of web presence, even if it's only a Facebook page, or a one page blog—you'll need as many people in your corner as possible, so use the Internet to its fullest potential

Learn as much as possible about the property you want to gain access to, whether public or private. What was the land originally used for and why has it become vacant? Quite often, large unused properties have turned into illegal dumps and hangouts. Explain to the property owner (or town officials) that allowing your club to utilize the land responsibly might help alleviate these issues. Offer to clean up the trash and monitor the property. On a more cautious note, be very careful about telling potential members of the property's location until you have permission to use it. As mentioned earlier, many members are only looking for a place to ride and couldn't care less about the club's long term existence.

Once you've found a few potential properties, put together a plan for dealing with the property owners, town officials, and adjoining neighbors. Anticipate problems, negativity, and roadblocks, and come up with viable solutions. The better prepared you are, the better your chances of success. Identify other potential trail users and try to think of a way for dirt bikes to share the space—this is more important if the parcel is public land as private property owners can decide who accesses their land and who doesn't. Research the recreational and liability laws of your State, as every private landowner will be concerned about safety and liability.

It would also be a good idea to have some type of financial plan in place. Even though your club is non-profit and run by volunteers, you'll still need money for insurance, maintaining the property, and supplying food for the monthly meeting (even if it's only coffee and cake). Membership dues, bake sales, club t-shirts, and raffle tickets are all good ways to generate income. Contact other clubs, even if they're not nearby and ask how they operate their club. Once your club has been in existence for a few years, you can start applying for some grant money.

Grant money: There is both public and private grant money available and the more applications you submit the better your chances of success. The biggest public grant program is the RTP (Recreational Trails Program). The RTP is part of an the Department of Transportation's Federal Highway Administration (FHWA) and provides funding to the individual States to develop and maintain recreational trails, and each State distributes the money to the various organizations. The grants are open to all clubs and organizations, so the competition for funds can be fierce.

Private grant money is available from Polaris Industries (an ATV manufacturer) and Yamaha Motorcycles. The Polaris program is known as T.R.A.I.L.S. (Trail Development, Responsible riding, Access, Initiatives, Lobbying and Safety). Polaris is an ATV manufacturer, so it's no surprise that most grants have been awarded to ATV clubs, but dirt bikes and ATVs usually share trails so it can't hurt to submit an application. Funds are normally used for trail development maintenance projects, safety or education programs, and lobbying efforts to keep access to off-road areas open.

Yamaha has a G.R.A.N.T program (Guaranteeing Responsible Access to our Nation's Trails). These grants provide funds for trail maintenance, rider safety, and trail mapping. Both grant programs are only for off-road clubs so the competition is not as bloodthirsty as it is for federal grant money. When trying to convince a property owner to allow access to his land, knowing there is grant money available to help maintain and even improve his property may tip the scales in your favor.

People skills: You'll also need to brush up on your people and public speaking skills as uncomfortable as that may be. Not everyone likes dirt bikes. There might be some hostile neighbors to deal with, and you may need to make a few presentations to the town board. A few of the typical community concerns are increased traffic, noise, dust, trespassing, and garbage. You'll need to have a plan to deal with those concerns. You should be able to answer these questions without thinking:

- who are you and your members
- who will manage the club and what qualifications do they have
- how will you keep people from going off the trails

- how will you deal with noise, parking and litter
- what are the hours and days of operation

If you can't answer those questions, you won't be taken seriously. Formulate a public presentation and practice it in front of family, friends, or even a mirror. Recruit someone to act the part of a hostile antagonist so you can get used to the stress of dealing with those situations. This way you won't get unnerved at a public meeting and either appear unprepared, or worse yet, lose your cool and start lashing out at your antagonist.

When trying to create a new off-road park, you're better off focusing on recreational trail riding in the beginning as opposed to racing. Once your club is established and has a proven track record for safe, responsible behavior, you can look into higher risk activities like competitive trail riding and motocross racing.

Most importantly—keep a positive outlook. The future of off-road recreation depends on our ability to assimilate into mainstream recreational society. Clubs are an essential and important component of that assimilation.

Chapter Nine:
The Future of Off-Road Recreation

"Treat the earth well. It was not given to you by your parents; it was loaned to you by your children." Kenyan proverb

Charles Darwin, the 19th century English naturalist is often quoted as saying "only the strong survive", but a more appropriate quote (credited to Leon Meggison) is . . . *"In the struggle for survival, the fittest win out at the expense of their rivals because they succeed in adapting themselves best to their environment".* Which, if applied to the dirt bike riders of today, can be loosely interpreted to mean that having a large population of off-road riders does count, but a greater asset for survival in today's recreational world is adaptability and the willingness of those riders to be active and proactive.

It has been estimated that the population of the United States will reach 438 million by the year 2050, up from 306 million in 2008. This new wave of humanity will need housing, hospitals, commerce, and schools. From a recreational standpoint, more development equals less open space, and less open space equals more competition for an already scarce resource (recreational land).

Our Struggle for Existence

Although Darwin was referring to plants and animals, many of his principles can be applied to land-use conflicts across the United States. If we consider each recreational group as an individual species, we can adjust Darwin's theory to see that each species (hikers, cyclists, equestrians, etc.) is competing for survival in the land-use struggle.

The Earth is finite and as resources dwindle (less open space) and demand intensifies (population explosion), our fight for dirt bike survival will escalate. How we deal with this conflict is up to us. We have to decide what we need to do to preserve the trails we already have access to, while working towards securing more trails for tomorrow's generation. In other words, how are we going to adapt in order to compete with other species for the limited resource of open space?

We need to adapt, compromise, negotiate, and strive to create a win-win situation with other recreational species in order to be able to share the space. We need to ask ourselves why other groups are successful in procuring lands for their use while we continue to lose acreage. We also need to take a long, hard, objective look at the reasons behind our constant struggle.

Off-road riding in Europe has a long, storied, almost noble history. We need to bring some honor and respect to our sport. Riding a dirt bike is not a right; it's a privilege, and privileges come with responsibilities. Excessive noise, trespass, damage to private property, and lack of cohesiveness are all battles we need to overcome from within the ranks. The oft-repeated refrain of "that's the way it's always been", especially when referring to tolerated areas is a dinosaur's attitude and if we don't change the tune, our fate will be the same as the dinosaurs: extinction.

Nothing is the way it was, nor does anything stay the same. The only constant is change. The same tolerated areas that were once local secrets have been whispered throughout locker rooms, boasted about in bars, and posted on enough Internet forums to make than common public knowledge. Nothing shuts down a riding area (especially a locally tolerated one) faster than overuse and irresponsible behavior. We need to focus on moving forward and leaving the past behind.

Looking Towards the Future

Getting involved is not difficult and can yield new friends and new places to ride. Join a club in your area, or if none exist, look into forming one. You can also join organizations, such as *The AMA* (American Motorcyclist Association), *The Blue Ribbon Coalition*, and *Tread Lightly*. These groups offer riders a united front on the Washington political scene and are dedicated to keeping off-road trails open to the public. Try writing polite, respectful letters to all your local politicians asking for help in obtaining a place to ride. If you already belong to a club and they ask you to attend a town board meeting, shut off the television and go.

Think Again

So you think dirt bikes can never be banned? Think again. If you're over the age of thirty-five, did you ever think they would be able to effectively ban smoking? Whether it's the CPSC (Consumer Product Safety Commission) attacking dirt bikes and ATVs for safety reasons, environmentalists laying claim to trails systems, or the Federal Government re-designating public lands as Wilderness, it all raises red flags for off-road enthusiasts.

Even if riding a dirt bike were a right, it's still not safe. The right to bear arms is cemented in our Bill of Rights so it's safe, correct? Maybe. You may still be able to own a gun, but what good is a gun without ammunition? Guns may be protected, but ammunition isn't. Dirt bikes may not be banned, but public riding areas can, will, and are, being shut down. You might own a dirt bike, but unless you own your own property, the bike may end up gathering dust in your garage.

Doom and gloom? Not really; just realistic observations. Please get involved so that we may pass the sport of dirt bikes on to the next generation of kids (and adults).

Chapter Ten:
A Few Basic Riding Tips

"You play as you practice." Red Auerbach

Although this book is not meant as a how-to-ride book, here are some basic riding tips for beginners.

For every action there is a reaction: Be careful of something called "whiskey throttle". If you twist the throttle too much, the bike will accelerate quickly, throwing your body backwards. This makes your hand twist more throttle which propels your body backwards even more until eventually, you and the bike part ways. Take the time to slowly acclimate yourself with any unfamiliar bike. Roll on the throttle instead of twisting it. The same with the brakes—there's no need to stomp or grab the brakes. Today's bikes are very sensitive to the touch. Easy does it.

Jump, jump and away: Once you decide you're ready to start jumping, the best advice for a beginner is to keep a steady throttle up to, over, and after the jump. Panic revving the throttle will make the front end of the bike come up, and if you chop (let off) the throttle, the nose will drop down and you can endo. Steady and consistent throttle control will win every time. Find a small jump and work your way up from there.

Heads up: Keeping your head up sounds simple, but it's a very difficult skill for beginners to master. Your body will follow your eyes, so if you keep looking at that big rock you're afraid of hitting, you're going to hit it without a doubt. Train yourself to look past obstacles because the farther ahead you look, the more time you will have to react to an unsafe condition. Keeping your eyes up to scan the horizon is one of the best ways to improve safety.

Poor man's riding course: If you don't have the money to buy instructional dirt bike DVDs, check out You Tube, but remember that anyone can post a video, so the person you're watching may not be a good rider—they just think they are. Try searching for some of the top pro riders and see if they've posted any videos.

Slow down to speed up: It sounds like a paradox, but sometimes you need to slow down to speed up. Learn the proper techniques and practice them until they're second nature. The speed will follow in due time. Riding a dirt bike requires a good amount of practice in the beginning stages. With age comes wisdom and patience, so use it!

Press, don't turn: Turning a dirt bike is more a matter of weight transition than an actual turning of the bars. Press the bars rather than turning them, and use your body weight to help balance the bike through a turn.

Legs, not arms: Keep your body central to the bike, grip with your legs, and let the bike move around you. Riding a dirt bike is much more about your legs than your arms.

Practice, practice, practice: Practice drills can be boring, but try to choose one drill and practice it for at least twenty minutes before starting to play ride.

Tree roots can fool you: Tree roots and logs are best traversed head on. Not head on as in full speed ahead, but in a straight line to the obstacle.

If you have to cross them at an angle, be ready for the back tire to slide sideways, especially on tree roots.

Ride within your limits: If something scares you, turn back, or go around the obstacle. Don't let an obstacle (or other riders) taunt your ego.

Rome wasn't built in a day: Learning to ride a dirt bike competently is a work in progress. You'll have good days and bad days. Don't get discouraged and don't be in a rush. Learn the basics and practice them over and over again until they are ingrained into your mind and body, and become second nature.

> Mountain biking is a great way to cross train for riding dirt bikes.

Chapter Eleven:
Glossary

"The wise speak only of what they know" Gandalf (Lord of the Rings)

Arenacross: A scaled down version of Supercross that is held in arenas as opposed to stadiums. The smaller course is tighter than a Supercross course and has even less room for errors. Technique and fitness are important components for winning.

Dual-sport bike: You can look at a dual-sport bike as a street legal dirt bike, or a street bike with off-road benefits. It's designed for both on and off-road use and is equipped with street-legal equipment such as headlight, taillight, turn signals, horn, mirrors, and street legal muffler.

Enduro: Sometimes called "the thinking man's (or woman's) race". It's actually more of a time keeping event than a race, as enduros do not rely on speed alone. The riders leave at timed intervals and there is a pre-determined time schedule riders must adhere to. The rider whose time matches the scheduled time the closest wins the event. Less crowded and frenetic than motocross or harescrambles.

Endurocross: Endurocross is a mix of supercross, trail, and motocross racing. The indoor course is a mix of natural and man-made obstacles. The track consists of rock gardens, fallen logs (or utility poles), water crossings, giant tires and boulders. Speed counts, but technique is important for getting over the obstacles without crashing.

Four stroke: An engine that relies on four strokes to complete a cycle of: a) intake fuel/air, b) compress the mixture, c) power down the piston, and d) exhaust. The four-stroke delivers a smooth broad range of power.

Hare and Hound: It's a full-on race that's run over a natural terrain course. It has a mass start and the first rider to cross the finish line wins. Similar to a harescramble, but longer and usually held out West which is why they are sometimes called desert races.

Harescramble: Raced on a marked loop course, usually through a wooded trail on natural terrain. The race is run for a designated number of laps or length of time (generally around two hours). Harescrambles use a mass start and are a full on race from start to finish. The first rider to cross the finish line wins.

Holeshot: The first person out the gate and through the first turn after the starting gate drops gets the holeshot.

Jumps: Since this is a beginner's guide, you may not know the names of each jump so they are all included here under the main heading of "jumps".

Single: All other jumps are based on the single jump which is basically a pile of dirt in the middle of the trail or course, and can vary in height.

Double: A double is two single jumps with a gap in between. The rider takes off on the front face of the first jump, and lands on the back face of the second jump. It sounds easy, but the degree of difficulty rises exponentially from a single jump to a double jump.

Triple: Three single jumps with a gap between each one. Riders jump the front face of the first jump, fly over the second jump, and land on the back face of the third jump. Not for inexperienced riders! One small miscalculation can lead to lots of pain and broken plastic.

Tabletop: If there is any such thing as a "safe" jump, the tabletop is it. It's basically a double jump, except the void between the jumps is filled in with dirt, creating a flat top similar to a table top. Or look at it as a flat jump with ramps at either end.

Knobby: Type of tire used in off-road riding. They get the name knobby because they have blocks of rubber (or knobbies) protruding up from the base of the tire to enable the bike to get traction on loose terrain. Kind of like cleats on a sport shoe.

Motocross: Motocross is a fast, physically demanding, visually spectacular, almost addictive riding discipline. Motocross races are held on an enclosed course that combines the terrain's natural features such as hills and cambers with man-made jumps. A typical motocross track will have many transitions and obstacles such as fast straights, steep hills and drops, big jumps, berms, ruts, and whoops. There is a mass start with a backwards dropping gate and the first rider to cross the finish line wins the race. Fast, furious and very competitive. It's as much an art form as it is a sport.

Motocross bike: Motocross is a specialized sport and the bikes they use are specialized bikes. They're lighter in weight than trail or dual-sport bikes and are known for their abrupt power delivery, which allows them to get the acceleration and high speeds needed to race competitively.

Motocross flags (in general):
- *Green:* race is a go, all is good
- *Yellow:* exercise caution
- *Black:* leave the race track and find the marshall
- *White:* one lap left to go
- *Checkered:* you've finished the race
- *Red:* stop all racing and stay in that spot until directed by a track official on where to go
- *Blue/orange:* move to the outside of the track
- *White/Red Cross:* ambulance and/or medical personnel on track, rider injured, slow down and maintain your position, no passing or jumping

Ignorance is no excuse. It's up to you to learn the safety and equipment rules of your riding area

Observed trials: Trials riders have been called the "violin players" of the off-road world due to the level of mastery of their machines. Observed trials are a unique off-road competition, which does not rely on speed. Trials competitors negotiate sections of extremely difficult and rugged terrain without touching the ground with any part of their body. Points are added for each mistake and the rider with the lowest score wins.

Supercross: A motocross-type race conducted inside stadiums on man-made tracks. The main event pits 20 riders for 20 laps. Tight turns, whoops sections, and big jumps make the action fast and competitive.

Trail bike: Tamer than a motocross bike, but lighter in weight and easier to handle off-road than a dual-sport bike. The four stroke models are quiet, very easy to ride, and the suspension is set up for long hours out on the trails.

Trials bike: Trials bikes are not designed for trail riding. The non-existent seat is a clear indication that sitting down is a very low priority for trials riders who stand on the foot pegs throughout the competition. The engine has an incredible amount of torque and very low gears so you can move at a low speed without having to worry about stalling.

Turkey Run: Follows a pre-determined route, but there is no timing and it's not a race. Can include on-road and off-road areas, so you'll probably need a street plate in most states.

Two stroke: Engines which rely on two strokes to complete a cycle of: a) intake fuel/air while powering down the piston, and b) compress the fuel/air and expending exhaust. The two-stroke delivers a snappy burst of power. Great bikes!

Whoops: A series of low piles of dirt that can be compared to moguls in skiing, except the whoops are on flat ground while moguls are on a downhill slope. The trick is to keep up enough speed so the front wheel stays on top of the piles and doesn't fall into the valleys. Whoops take a lot of practice. Mastering the intricacies of timing, throttle control, and body positioning are essential for getting through without crashing.

Chapter Twelve:

Resources

"We thought that we had the answers, it was the questions we had wrong." Bono of U2

Any directory always tries to include the most up to date information but as you may imagine, resources continually change. They move, refocus, sometimes shut their doors, or dismantle their website. The only guarantee in life is change, so check the information for accuracy. The links were accurate and live at press time. The following list is only the tip of the iceberg as far as links are concerned. Spend a rainy afternoon on the Internet just searching around for different off-road related websites. There is also a companion website for this book at www.dirtbikes101.com that has more links and resources.

Safety Gear: (you knew that would first, right?)

We'll couple safety gear and off-road gear together since most stores sell both.

http://www.motocrossgiant.com/

http://www.motosport.com/

http://www.rockymountainatv.com/home.do

http://www.bobscycle.com/

http://www.motorcycle-superstore.com/

Amazon.com also sells safety gear and off-road accessories.

Safety Courses:

Motorcycle Safety Foundation:
http://www.msf-usa.org/
This is the main page for the Street Rider Course and you can also purchase their DVDs and other accessories here.

MSF Dirt Bike School:
http://www.dirtbikeschool.com/

For returning riders who have some experience, look into: **Shane Watts Dirt Wise School:**

http://www.shanewatts.com.

(Shane's school isn't appropriate for absolute beginners—you must have some off-road experience.)

Bike Manufacturers:

Honda:
  http://powersports.honda.com

Kawasaki:
  http://www.kawasaki.com/Home/Home.aspx

KTM:
  http://www.ktm.com

Suzuki:
  http://www.suzukicycles.com/

Yamaha:
  http://www.yamaha-motor.com/

Dirt Bike Magazines:

Dirt Rider:
http://www.dirtrider.com/

Dirt Bike:
http://www.dirtbikemagazine.com/

Transworld Motocross:
http://motocross.transworld.net/

Dirt Bike DVDs:

You may not be familiar with the names of the top riders that have training DVDs on the market, so here's a list of names you can search for, but the DVDs are aimed at novice/advanced beginners. Only the MSF DVD is for total beginners.

Shane Watts
Gary Semics
Ryan Hughes
Jeremy McGrath
MSF (Beginners Guide)
Stefan Everts

It's not an instructional DVD as far as how to ride is concerned, but it's an amazing story that covers some amazing terrain, and visits some amazing places that most Americans would never see

otherwise. It's Ewan McGregor and Charlie Boorman in **Long Way Round and Long Way Down.**
http://www.longwayround.com/journeys.htm

Off-Road Organizations:

NOHVCC (National Off-Highway Vehicle Conservation Council): http://www.nohvcc.org/ The NOHVCC offers excellent resources on starting a club and other off-road activities:

AMA (American Motorcyclist Association): http://www.ama-cycle.org/

Tread Lightly:
http://www.treadlightly.org/

Bureau of Land Management:
http://www.blm.gov/ca/st/en/prog/recreation/ohv.html

American Trails.org:
http://www.americantrails.org/

U.S. Forest Service:
http://www.fs.fed.us/recreation/programs/ohv/

Regional Organizations:

Try searching for Off-Road Rider Associations in your state. Here are a few to give you an idea:

ECEA (East Coast Enduro Association):
http://www.ecea.org/ecea/index.php?act=home

SETRA (South Eastern Enduro and Trail Riders Association:
http://www.setra.org/setraorg/default.aspx

NETRA (New England Trail Riders Association):
http://www.netra.org/

NATRA (North Alabama Trail Riders Association):
http://www.natra-westpoint.net/TopicsMain.php

NYSORV (New York State Off-Highway Recreational Vehicle Association):
http://www.nysorva.info/
GOR (Georgia Off-Road):
http://www.georgiaoffroad.com/

Discussion Forums:

Your regional discussion forum is a great resource, but there are other general dirt bike forums that are also a good source of information.

For Honda owners there is CRF's Only:
http://www.crfsonly.com/catalog/index.php

KTM owners have KTM Talk:
http://ktmtalk.com/index.php

There is also **Thumper Talk**, which now covers both two stroke and four stroke bikes, but they began mainly as a four stroke (thumper) forum.
http://www.thumpertalk.com/

For dual sport bikes, visit **ADV Rider** (Adventure Rider)
http://www.advrider.com/
Also try doing a search using each manufacturer's name (i.e., "honda dirt bike forum", etc). This will lead to other forums such as KDX rider.net, kawiforums, etc.

Miscellaneous:

Some search words to use might be: dirt bike clubs (followed by your state), places to ride dirt bikes (followed by your state), off-road trail maps, motocross tracks, harescrambles, enduro, supercross, WORCS, ISDE, arenacross, GNCC,

Chapter Twelve

Outdoor Nationals, and OHV (off highway vehicle) trails.

Cross check for trail systems by substituting the letters ATV (all terrain vehicle) for dirt bike, since many of the trails are used by both ATVs and dirt bikes.

Author's Note:

There are no wrong turns in life—some turns just take you the long way around. Think of your life as your own personal motocross track. There are bumps, ruts and blind turns. There are also long stretches of easy straight sections. You won't get the checkered flag every time out of the gate, but anyone making it around the course is a winner!

Hopefully you've gleaned some helpful hints from this book. If you think riding dirt bikes is something you'd enjoy, don't wait too long to get started. It's a big decision and it takes time to do the research.

I wish each and every one of you the very best of luck and many long years in the saddle. Stay safe, be happy, give thanks, and above all—enjoy Life! ☺

Chris Carragher
www.dirtbikes101.com

5919269R00083

Printed in Great Britain
by Amazon.co.uk, Ltd.,
Marston Gate.